WHY DON'T YOU WANT MY STUFF?

A Boomer's guide to downsizing, their Millennial

kids' psyche and just things that are so...

JOSH LEVINE

Why don't you want my stuff?
Copyright © 2017 Josh Levine

ISBN (Print Edition): 978-1-54392-199-1
ISBN (eBook Edition): 978-1-54391-684-3

INTRODUCTION

It seems to be one of the most common questions adult children are asked today by their aging parents, "Why don't you want my stuff?" The parent is frustrated. The child is frustrated. Neither knows what to do with a household of antique and vintage collectibles including fine dining china, art, crystal, silver, Hummels, baseball cards and other items collected over a lifetime.

As a certified auctioneer and appraiser with close to 20 years of experience, I see this constantly and I just wanted to get to the bottom of it. This trend and question has become more and more common each and every year. Parents who are downsizing ask me, "Can you believe my kids don't want this?" And I'm kind of surprised, and happy they don't. We auctioneers used to have to fight off the family members for the antiques and collectibles in a house. It was inevitable and even after we signed a contract to liquidate an estate, some long-lost family member would turn up just to grab a "few things" that they wanted before the auction. A few minutes later, all the valuables were gone. I used to call the extended family "the locust." This was because of their voracity for picking a nice estate auction clean before we got to conduct the sale.

As auctioneers we don't charge a fee, but rather we are paid commission. So, we want to have nice assets to sell. When we are left with the Tupperware and towels there is no money left in it for us. Now this has completely flipped to the point where I am asking myself, "Why doesn't anyone in the family want this?" Not that I am complaining, mind you. Quite the contrary -- our business has been booming with fresh to the market estate items, many of which have been in families for multiple generations. These once treasured heirlooms passed from generation to generation are now looked upon as a burden.

The younger generations are not interested. I constantly hear them say, "Where am I going to store that?" "It's not my taste." "It doesn't fit my décor."

The parents don't understand, and often are hurt by their children's rejection of their valued collectibles. I have seen actual anger and bad blood over these issues.

It's my sincere hope that this book enlightens both sides in this interesting trend. You will find that it's not new historically, and there are a few good scientific, psychological rationales. I also hope you, your children and other relatives learn something and we can bridge the gap of understanding of the larger issues and market trends. I also believe, like George Carlin, "It's just stuff, so don't get so caught up in it." Relationships are so much more important than stuff. As a child of hoarders and raised by children of the Depression, I saw firsthand how stuff can be so important. I am sure it's why I do what I do for a living and I am in fact a minimalist. Don't tell anyone that! So, let's get started and see what we can both learn about the trends, each other and get all Nostradamus.

THE SECONDARY MARKET: IT'S A BUYER'S MARKET AND WILL BE FOR SOME TIME

Auctions, yard sales, estate sales, thrift stores, consignment shops, eBay, Amazon and Etsy. Okay I'll say it, classified ads too. They all are the secondary market and where you should be shopping. To say there are deals is an understatement. The Baby Boomers are the largest generation by population and they're moving into retirement. Unlike their predecessors, The Greatest Generation, they are taking control of their destinies and selling now. To top it off, the overall trend is towards minimalism or in layman's terms, people are downsizing.

What am I saying? The World War II generation passed down their family heirlooms as the generation before them had. I often hear from the Boomers that they "don't want to do that to their kids." I know what they mean. They speak of the overwhelming task they undertook with the loss of their parents and loved ones. Dealing with the often multiple estates that were in their parents' homes was a burden to them. Then they were tasked with disposing, selling and passing on to other relatives. Did I mention the family fights yet?

I hear their stress and emotions when they tell me the stories of dealing with all of this. They take off work for several weeks, never being right in the eyes of relatives that, mind you, aren't helping, and in the end had a bad overall experience. Out of this they have decided, now 20 years later, to not burden anyone with this undertaking and have said, "Sell it." They tend to be realists and more informed to current resale values. They want you to buy it so they don't burden anyone with it. This generation actually fought over the stuff when their parents passed or downsized. Again this is why it means so much to them, and why they are so hurt when their kids don't want the family china, piano and other items, or get what all the fuss is about.

Now we are on to the next problem. The current "buying" generations with disposable income don't want anything. They are minimalists. iPhones and a new app aside, something used or antique... no. That's gross! Here we have a large supply, no demand. I am full circle to the Buyer's Market and the subject of my ramblings. It's a perfect storm for a Buyer's Market.

Here's what I do know. This is nothing new. What? Yes, these trends repeat in cycles. In the roaring 20s, and with a Devil-may-care, frivolous attitude, we bought new. In the 1950s and 1960s, we went to Sears and bought new as well. Today, the best-kept secret is the secondary market. If you are a collector, the world is your oyster. And, I believe, a great long-term investment. I truly think these uninterested people will get nostalgic in their later years. They will want what they remember their parents or grandparents having. We all tend to get nostalgic when we get older, and we are living longer than ever. We are just too busy with life to care right now. But, spending some time exploring the secondary market now could pay off big-time in the future!

AN INTERESTING SIDE NOTE ON MINDSET

I often share, okay... overshare and while doing so I recently received some amazing feedback. It's funny how when you listen to people, a skill I try very hard to work on, they will teach you something.

I was talking in the lobby of our auction gallery about my plans to write this book. I elaborated on all my theories when the young woman I was talking to told me why she didn't want her parents' stuff. Ready for it? She said she and most people her age don't want your stuff because they resent it. The word she used was 'hate.' I don't know too many people that collect things they hate.

Okay... let me explain, as it was explained to me. Her mother would constantly warn her and her brother, "Don't touch that, you'll break it." "That is not a toy, that was your grandmother's." "Put that down! Do you know how much that's worth?"

On and on until it made her hate that piece. It wasn't fun, and it wasn't something she would ever want to collect. It almost ruined all antiques for her.

Psychologically it makes sense. I know because it gave me flashbacks. I heard all of those same things. She was pretty self-aware and in tune because she further explained that her mother loved antiques. Her mother had fond memories of playing with these things as a little girl. Her grandmother let her mom play with them, because to her, they were utilitarian and to be used. Mom had fond memories and love for these objects, and because of the emotions they evoked as an adult she wanted to protect them from a clumsy child who didn't understand their perceived value.

Instead of letting her daughter build a sentimental attachment too, she created a hatred for this fragile thing her daughter wasn't allowed to touch. Is all of this too Freud for you? By the way, Mom's not a bad person for this and I do not judge a generation that probably had a lot of moms like this in it. Just like my mom and most I can remember.

WHAT THE MILLENNIAL DOESN'T KNOW

I know what you're thinking -- this young generation already knows every-thing. I used to know everything too. What I do know, and they don't, is that they are going to become collectors.

Did you hear a gasp? Say it isn't so! I'll never collect anything. And I say yes, yes you will. You just don't know what it is and when it's going to hap-pen to you, but it happens to just about everyone.

Let me explain further. The Greatest Generation collected hand-me-downs, heirlooms, had hope chests, liked trinkets and bobbles. They had babies at 17. Their kids were grown and out of the house before they were 38. They found themselves grandparents at age 40 with disposable income in the 1950s. They were 40-year-old collectors.

Move forward to the Baby Boomers. Married out of college, had babies in their early 20s, their kids went to college and they had disposable income after paying for that college at 50. They were the largest generation, so they collected a lot of stuff. Stay with me Millennial, as I know your atten-tion span has waned after I mentioned a few curse words, like antiques and collectibles, but here comes the affliction. You are getting married at 30, having kids at 38 and will be paying for their school and health care until you are 65, and then it will hit you. "I want to collect something and I can't help myself." You will also live longer, so you'll be buying all sorts of stuff you don't need. You won't pull "my mom" and shop on QVC all day, but you'll have an Amazon hologram in your living room asking, "What can our drones bring you this afternoon?" But, I digress and hope you see my line of logical thinking. Let's talk about something else to wash off how that felt to the Millennials. I am sure your parents are now gloating as they read on, and think, "You'll be sorry you didn't keep your grandmother's china." Oh, don't worry, I'll talk china and China later. Let's beat up on your parents a little in the next section.

WHEN SELLING, DON'T BE FOOLED BY YOUR PRICE ANCHOR

What is a price anchor? Oh, let me tell you my friends. A price anchor occurs when someone you trust tells you the value of something based on perceived value from the past. It could be something your grandmother told you when you were a child. It could be your dying aunt on her death bed in Madagascar, whispering in your ear and spoken like an end-of-times prophecy. This is how you generate the value of something you are going to inherit. There is your anchor and the price comes from the false perception that what they said has more validity than the facts.

Here is a real, paraphrased story, as told to me by a wonderful consignor. "My great grandmother told me that she used to date Edgar Degas. She was a dancer at the time in France. She brought one of his paintings to the U.S. on a plane long ago and even had to charter its own seat as it was so large and baggage claim would not allow it underneath."

This was now the word of God or Great Grandma to a young girl. Here was her price anchor and $10 million parachute retirement. It sounded awesome to me and as a novice auctioneer at the time I was all in. I jumped in the ocean holding onto the anchor as well.

I contacted several experts who were equally excited. I told them the legend, sent them photos and waited for them to tell me how I was about to make my name in the business for finding this rare treasure. Then a wonderful gentleman and French Impressionist expert let me have it eloquently and plainly. He showed me how the work was not an original, but an early 20th century printing technique and saw how I, a novice, could be fooled. He showed me which actual work it was a copy of. He then talked me off the ledge, or in this case, the bottom of the sea as I was holding the price anchor.

Now the hard part. I had to tell the consignor and her family that the legend was not true. Did you see it coming? The messenger was shot. I was the idiot and they were convinced they had a valuable and original Degas. They were going to New York to sell it at a major auction house and I was a fool, or worse trying to pull something. I took it very personally. Funny thing is that now, so many years later, it's so common in my business and if a consignor doesn't want to let go of their price anchor I just pleasantly pass on the items.

Truth be told, sometimes time is the anchor. What people were told at the time may have been true. The value could have been there, but tastes change and now there may be no interest or demand. Age doesn't matter in the end – it all boils down to desirability. You can show someone 100 sales results for the exact thing they have, be it on eBay, Invaluable, Live

Auctioneers or auction records worldwide and it won't matter. Mom, Dad or Great Grandma gave them the price anchor and it is THE TRUTH.

CYCLICAL TRENDS: SHOULD YOU HANG ON TO MOM'S CHINA SET?

Now let's get to my negative folks who believe the world of antiques and collectibles is done, never to be seen again. Are all collectors dead? Will there be an app for keepsakes and thingamabobs? Will people collect rare emojis? I don't know or think so, but we have seen a trend as Baby Boomers age and the current era of innovation changes our lifestyles, particularly among younger generations. We in the auction business thought Steampunk or Shabby Chic might be the movements to save the antique store, but that has not seemed to happen. However, as said before, I do think there will be a renewed interest in antiques as the world market shrinks and the long-term investor and collector realizes that we have been through this all before.

Cycles, trends, hills and valleys... we have seen this in the stock market, world market and heck even Halley's comet comes back to visit. An example for you pessimists is fine china. Take a set of 18th century Meissen, 19th century Limoges and 1950s Noritake. Did I just speak a foreign language to you? Well, those are makers of fine porcelain china sets from the 1700s, 1800s and 1900s. Each in their day commanded major bucks.

My mother once threatened to kick me out of the house after I broke a Noritake Azalea teacup. It was the 1970s and I was jamming to Kiss's 'Love Gun' album and the teacup vibrated off the table. Crazy Glue be damned, it was busted and so was I. At that time, prior to replacements.com, a popular website that offers replacements for old and new china, crystal and silver it was $300. Today, that same teacup can be purchased as a "Buy It Now" for $4.50 on eBay.

All the aforementioned porcelains can be purchased today for pennies on the dollar because we, as a society, are "just not doing that sort of thing" right now. Not even with 18th century treasures. We just are too busy to present a meal in the style of the ages from which I speak. Right now, that is. The Victorian era saw these huge china sets and their grand formality. The 1950s saw its return, and because I am Nostradamus, until proven otherwise, I think the 2030s will be its return. I kid, of course, because I am not French; however history and antique trends tend to repeat over and over again. Doubt me? Look around at the spring fashions this year: bell-bottoms are back again and I just saw a man with a fanny pack on at New York Fashion Week. Terrifying. Enough said. The long-term investor might just be at your mom's yard sale right now.... stealing the china set for $50. And regarding that yard sale, let's get in some tips. If you are finding yourself going through this process of selling, downsizing or help-ing someone do so, I did promise some education in here, so let's give it a shot. And if at any time while reading this book you notice I have writing ADD put the book down, turn on HGTV and watch a house flip show then pick the book back up and we should be back on track.

5 TIPS FOR THE DOWNSIZING BOOMER

Do you find yourself minimizing? Are you worried about leaving a legacy of clutter? Or, maybe you have parents who are of the age where it's time to downsize? By the way, I am sure you know your kids love you, but having them help you downsize and hearing they don't want any of your stuff will be quite exhausting. Remember this is just as hard on them as it is on you. It can really, as the Ancient Greeks would have said, suck!

You're not alone. A recent U.S. Census Bureau report in June 2015 states that there are 75.4 million Baby Boomers. Not surprisingly, Millennials who were born between 1982 and 2000 now outnumber the Boomers at 83.1 million. We're in a generational shift and the trend is clear: Boomers need to get rid of their stuff.

By definition, Baby Boomers were born between 1946 and 1964. Many in this demographic just recently dealt with liquidating their parents' estates. Some are retiring and others are reinventing themselves. Still others are making plans to travel the world while they can. They may be downsizing to simplify their lives or in an effort to not burden their kids – who don't want their household belongings – they are looking at ways to sell their valuables.

If you see yourself in this scenario, let me give you some tips:

1. **Research the secondary market.** Go to an auction and see what similar pieces sell for. Look on sites like eBay, Live Auctioneers and Invaluable. They will all let you search past sold items with a few clicks

of the mouse. In many cases you will be surprised by the values both in good ways and disheartening ways. Don't shoot the messenger -- it's just the law of supply and demand. You Boomers have a lot of stuff and the demand has dwindled, but I am not a downer or Negative Nancy. I just want to brace you.

2. **Ask your friends.** Don't be shy. Many people have gone through this recently and have valuable insight. Liquidating an estate can seem overwhelming, but it doesn't have to be. Friends who have gone through the process can share tips and referrals. There is now an entire new industry of professionals dedicated to just assisting in this process. I think of them as your kids you don't fight with.

3. **Call a licensed appraiser**. Many will offer their opinions for free, or at least on their initial consultation. Keep in mind that an appraisal certificate from many years ago can need updating as the market changes. Feel free to seek a few opinions. Not all of us appraisers are experts on everything. Your mind will rest easy when you have had the same story from two or more experts.

4. **Hit the local antique and consignment stores.** Check out those tags. It's a free education. Don't make the mistake of having a yard sale without knowing what you are doing. Mark my words, "You will give something away." I used to make a living going to yard and estate sales. I couldn't sleep at night and always felt guilty because I'd buy valuable items at a fraction of what they were worth. It's why I do what I do now.

5. **Remember that it's only stuff.** This is the hardest to remember. In the grand scheme of things you and your family are the most important thing. These "things" are, as George Carlin would say, "Just stuff." Have I quoted him twice already? Quite the man and 300 years from now scholars will probably look at some of his takes on humanity as science, like Freud. Anyway, as I said earlier, I was raised in a house by parents who would have made amazing stars on the popular A&E Show, *Hoarders*. I have seen what it's like to be attached to things, and all of the emotions that go with it. I am sure it is why I do what I do and why I often feel like a psychologist.

So really what I'm saying is educate yourself, ask questions, consult an expert, window shop and brace yourself

DON'T THROW THAT AWAY

If there is one thing that makes me cringe, it's when I visit a home to assess the value of estate items and the homeowner says, "I had a dumpster come in before you got here and threw away all of the junk." It's inevitable that the family tossed out something of value that really would have a big draw to the auction and collectors abroad. I tell anyone that will listen: don't throw away anything until you have a professional examine it.

One of my favorite stories to illustrate this point goes back many years, when I was called to a home to look at a deceased uncle's coin collection in Quakertown, PA. I sat at the kitchen table with the husband and wife, took a few minutes to review the set and came up with a value of approximately $1,000. They didn't seem surprised or excited by its value and thanked me.

While still seated, the husband went to fetch a bayonet and the wife went to get a glass of water. As I waited, I glanced at the waste paper basket at my feet and noticed a stack of old postcards and hunting licenses in the garbage. Resisting temptation to dig in the trash, I politely asked if I could go through the trash upon the wife's return. She looked puzzled, but agreed. I was like a kid in a candy store. There were vintage Halloween postcards and old Pennsylvania hunting licenses.

"You have quite a fine little ephemera collection here. What are you going to do with these?" I asked. They looked at me like I was nuts. I then told them that their little pile was worth more than the coin collection. Now I had their attention. I asked if I could auction the hunting licenses and postcards for them. Of course, the answer was "Sure!"

Well, they were quite pleased with the results. The hunting licenses realized more than $3,000 with one selling for $950 alone. The postcards brought close to $2,000. I remember getting them more than $5,000 for the contents of the trash can.

I must be honest. These were very rare and fine examples and not all hunting licenses and postcards have significant value, but it illustrates my point well. After the auction, I learned that they tossed their uncle's old books, car manuals, old tractor catalogs and more.

I remember another situation in Souderton, PA when we went to look at some antique furniture and the clients had also brought in a dumpster. Glancing in it before the summer downpour ensued, I saw vintage papers and postcards that were laid on top and had gotten soaked and ruined. I didn't have the heart to tell them, but I had a pit in my stomach as the rain kept coming for three days. I wondered what treasures were in there... the history, the collectibles, the "money" that was being flooded. I often shudder to think what the value was of what was now in the Bucks County Landfill. Call me a Drama Queen.

Back to the first family, I didn't dwell on it or tell them, but believe they had a clue from my line of questions. Two weeks later when they got their check, they thanked me and have since referred our business to others. Oddly, they never gave me the coin collection to sell. Go figure. I have hundreds of stories, all similar. That may be my sequel, *An Auctioneers Tale*. In the movie I'll of course be played by Brad Pitt or David Beckham, if he could ever work on his acting chops. But, let me tell you another one or two stories in the meantime.

HOW ONE PAINTING IN A GARAGE REALIZED $110,000

This is a story about a rare find that almost went unfound and it happened recently in an unassuming neighborhood in metro Phoenix.

We were contacted by a consignor and his power of attorney who needed help cleaning out a home in the large retirement community of Sun City. The call was about a Michael Jordan poster and they just wanted to make sure that there wasn't anything of value in the home before they cleaned it out for sale. The gentleman was moving into an assisted living facility. This is a common call for our firm. Upon visiting the home, my consignment specialist noticed an unusual painting in the garage, one that most people might have ignored. And once again, a dumpster was waiting in the yard for the "junk" to be thrown out.

But this was no ordinary painting. Rather than a square or rectangular canvas, this painting was shaped as a diamond that was flipped on its side and measured 24.5" x 98.5" x 1.75". And no, this was not a portrait or a landscape. Instead, there were three large acrylic bands of black, green and yellow across the diamond canvas. The artist, Kenneth Noland, had entitled it "Replace!".

When I first saw the painting, I had a hunch it could be authentic. Noland was an American painter, who was renowned for Color Field painting and a key figure in the Post-Painterly Abstraction movement. The more I researched Noland, the more excited I got. His "Circle" piece realized more than $2.1 million at a 2013 Christie's auction.

So, why would one of his paintings be in Sun City and how come no one knew about it? Sadly, the owner of the painting was not well and we were unable to talk with him. But, with the help of his neighbor and dear friend, we could piece together the provenance. We had the name of the painting's previous owner and contacted the Kenneth Noland archive hoping to learn more. The Noland archive confirmed that this previous owner - a woman - was gifted the Noland in 1980, which then led us to our next questions. Who was she and why was she gifted such a serious piece of art? After contacting various New York galleries we learned that she was a part of the inner circle of New York's most prominent modern artists by way of Clement Greenberg. The connection to Sun City? She was the owner's sister.

Fast forward to a few days before the auction. The art world got wind of what we had and online views and bids were heating up. On auction day, I had a really good feeling about the interest in this piece. It came up for auction late in the day, but did not disappoint. I opened it up at $65,000 and before long we had floor, online and phone bidders bringing the price up higher and higher. A phone bidder from New Jersey was the winner, paying $110,000 for the rare piece.

I truly believe that because we were able to examine items at the home many valuable pieces were saved from that dumpster and in fact at the time of writing this, we are still working on proving the authenticity of another piece of art from this same collection. I smell another book. For now, let me tell another story about a potential dumpster and really about getting a second opinion.

WHEN A $5,000 OFFER IS TOO GOOD TO BE TRUE

Sometimes the rush and stress of settling a parent's estate makes people in vulnerable positions do what in hindsight, is a crazy thing.

A few years back now, I received a phone call from a gentleman in Colorado who was interested in getting our opinion regarding the value of the contents of his mother's home. He had received an offer of $5,000 for the contents of his mother's trailer in a senior living community in Mesa, Arizona and wanted to make sure he was not being taken advantage of.

The trailer itself was estimated to worth $30,000. Upon calling a firm that buys out contents of estates he received a cash offer for a buy-out. He really liked the fact that by accepting the $5,000 flat fee he could be rid of the contents and get the house on the market quickly. This is a common misnomer, as many times heirs see the real estate as the big value regarding the estate. Many large trust departments do this very same thing. Not seeing the value in the collections or other assets but the big two: the bank account and the real estate.

Now back to the trailer, I didn't expect much as this man said most of the contents was junk. Several times he apologized before I even stepped foot in the front door for "probably wasting my time." And again, he had a 30-yard dumpster in the driveway as he was planning to throw much of it away. Note to self, buy a dumpster company. He also was concerned the house was a mess and explained that his mother was hoarding. Most don't realize to an auctioneer, hoards make us like kids in a candy store. I assured him that it would take a lot to shock me and I was thrilled to have a look.

Upon entry into the living room, I saw what looked like 19th century Germany. What struck me first were the .800 sterling German candelabras and then the sterling silver champagne buckets and bronze work. I immediately assessed that the $5,000 offer was more than "a little low."

Then I did something I rarely do in the auction business -- I personally guaranteed he'd net over $25,000 for the items at auction. Public auctions are never a guarantee, but I felt that the value I saw in just a sampling of items from the house was more than enough. Plus, I had not even dug into the drawers, closets and dumpster yet. I had explained to the client earlier that if I would have seen just $10,000 or so worth of items I'd suggest he take the $5,000, as it was a sure thing and an auction is not always predictable. But that was not the case. It turned out through the dig and pleasant conversation with the son, his father was a well-decorated Colonel during World War II. The house kept revealing his story and history with medals, helmets, accommodations and uniforms.

To make a wonderful and long story short, we were able to gross more than $65,000 from his items at auction. A much better story than the $5,000 offer he had received.

Bringing in an educated appraiser or auctioneer may save you from losing tens of thousands of dollars in the end. I'd be very cautious when the person you brought in for help wants to buy it. I don't want to paint with a broad brush as I do know many honorable estate buy-out people, but they should be vetted. There are many unscrupulous ones out there. Get several opinions before making such a big decision.

I told you about a few fun treasure stories, but now let me tell you about a few crazies with unrealistic expectations and families fighting over next to nothing.

YOU CAN'T SPLIT THAT CAR, PAINTING OR PITCHER IN HALF

As some of you are faced with liquidating your parent's estate, several challenges arise and most of them are family. Brothers and sisters, a few distant cousins, an evil nephew and throw in a touch of the dreaded daughter-in-law and... boo! Scared now, aren't you?

One of my favorite auction adages is, "It's easier to split money than it is stuff." I have seen many a family fight over things that would shock and amaze you.

Years ago in Hellertown, Pennsylvania a 47-year-old brother and a 42-year-old sister met with their individual lawyers in their deceased mother's very modest home. Enter me, a green auctioneer and appraiser, asked by the administrator of the will to oversee a fair and equitable split of a few items the siblings disagreed over. It sounded simple. After all, there was not much in the house.

It seemed civil, but odd and then a nerve was touched. I valued a Waterford Crystal pitcher at $300. The sister thought it was priceless and the brother wanted it. A few choice words came and then a fist that sent sister to the ground like they were four-year olds. I was speechless. The two attorneys were as well. We witnessed a physical assault over a pitcher. I broke up the fight by threatening to smash it. I explained they could each go to Macy's to buy one. This was not a rare family heirloom. It still had the label on it. I couldn't leave fast enough. I thought, "Crazy." I never thought I'd see anything like that again.

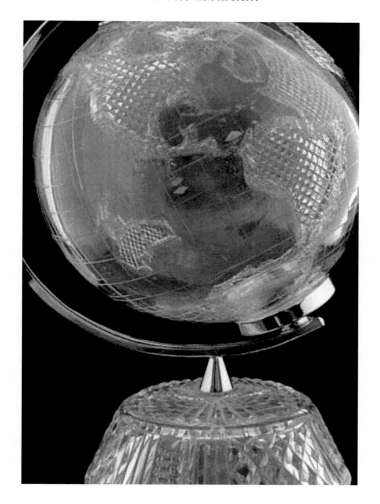

Fast forward many years and now I have seen most all of it. Unfortunately, it is something we see often. I remember a few of them by special names, like the "The Fighting Sisters." They would argue, fight, micromanage and cry every time I was at the house and all over just plain old stuff. Then there were "The Evil Twins" that lived on opposite sides of the country for good reason. These identical twins met at mom's estate, having not spoken in 10 years and after that process, I bet they won't speak again. Another is "The Sister-in-Laws Have Claws." Two peaceful, loving brothers brought their better halves to the property to split and I wanted to split! The boys didn't care about "the stuff," but their wives did.

I tell you these stories to help prepare, not scare you. Also, I just realized that other than the jerk-brother punching his sister, the other tales were all about the ladies. I apologize -- they were the ones that came to mind first. Men are just as awful in these situations. Now that I dredged my brain, I remember the "equitable" split of a family in Easton, PA. Each child could take one or two things and then the rest would be auctioned and split evenly. Makes sense. Big Sis took a clock, about $300. Little sis took a set of china and then came the brother. He just wanted a "simple bench," that he had covered with a blanket.

Everyone else removed their items from the house before we arrived, except for brother. He just kept mentioning not to take the piece under the blanket. When we were done cleaning out the three-story historic row home along the Delaware River, I just had to peek at the piece. Again, thinking it was a bench I wasn't concerned, but I had to look.

Turned out his pick from the house was by Roycroft. Quite rare and I was wowed by it. I was really chomping at the bit to start a family fight because I thought it was worth about $10,000 and he was getting one over on his sisters. I decided just to drop it, move on and not blow up a family. The bombshell of the story is I saw the same bench years later sell at auction for $190,000.

One way to avoid these uncomfortable, often tense scenarios, is to sell your personal collections while you still have a say. Or, by simply asking your kids what they want you can diffuse a future issue. If you're an heir, before you close your eyes and imagine punching your brother or wrestling your sister-in-law, remember – it's only stuff. If you're concerned that someone is taking more than his or her fair share, have a third-party professional evaluate the items to ensure everything will be equitable. Try to keep your emotions under control. It's hard to do, but it's the right thing.

WHEN TO SELL? WHAT'S HOT AND WHAT'S NOT

I am often asked, "When is the best time to sell my collection?" And not to be one accused of keeping my opinions to myself I say, "Strike while the iron is hot."

What do I mean by that? When you see record prices happening, sell your collection. Sounds obvious to most, but so often I hear, "I'll hold on to it. It can only go up from here," or "Imagine what it will be worth 20 years from now!" I don't know if it's prospecting, greed, or something their parents ingrained in these collectors, but I think it's a losing bet. Let me cite a few examples.

Fifteen years ago, we were selling Hummel collections and prices were riding high. I would see collections in my travels and ask folks if they wished to consign for auction and more often than not the owners would decline. Their consensus was that this would never end and Hummel's would keep increasing in value. Then about 10 years ago large collections began to be sold off and we could see it coming quickly. The crash. The collectors blamed the economy and kept waiting... and waiting... it wasn't the economy, but simple economics. Huge supply in this case and no demand from the next generation. I have yet to meet a Gen X'er or Millennial that collects them. Most have no idea what they are.

The next example is toy trains. A Pre-War Lionel train set was money in the bank for a long run. They were desired by many collectors and enthusiasts spanning several generations. They all had a train set when they were kids and had many fond memories of them. They sold like hot cakes and there were many serious collectors. Over the past five years toy collectors' tastes have changed and you can see the Hummel trend happening. A 2003 price of $12,000 for a Lionel Pre-War set is now $1,500 if you are lucky.

Some say it was video games that caused the younger generations to lose interest and that really may be true. I am actually surprised there's not a subset of Gen Xer's called the Atari Generation or Nintendo Generation.

What to do now? If you are thinking of selling a collection, sell it when it's hot. What is hot in toys? Star Wars toys from 1977 through 1984 as well as most action figures from this period. Also, Hot Wheels Redlines and AFX Aurora Slot Cars from the late 1960s through the early 1970s. Let me give you my forecast. Star Wars is going to peak with each new movie release. It's a great time to sell your Star Wars collectibles. Hot Wheels and Slot Cars are more urgent to sell as I feel they are going to go the way of the train set soon. I hate when I see a collection that was just held onto a little too long. It's just like playing the stock market, but when they fall off the cliff they don't recover to former glory.

The 80s toys you should be selling soon are He-Man, She-Ra, Transformers, Thundercats, Teenage Mutant Ninja Turtles and the like. I believe they may have all peaked and without a major successful movie soon their future interest may just become a footnote.

It makes sense, as the next generation of collectors won't know who these characters even are. If you think I am wrong, ask an 18-year-old who Woody Woodpecker is. They may giggle first, but trust me, they don't know. Even Popeye's legend is fading. The cats like Garfield, Heathcliff and Felix are all becoming blips of pop culture's radar. As for Tom and Jerry, they don't even know who Tom and Jerry are.

IT'S A BRAVE NEW WORLD

Embrace the world market if you are a seller, collector or buyer. If you have noticed, the world is shrinking. Don't panic, only figuratively. I am not going to insult your intelligence with the obvious. Okay, I am in this next line, but stay with me. The emergence of the Internet has changed the resale market drastically. I know, you're thinking thanks Josh, knew that. But I want to further explain the logic and simple economics that might have escaped you.

When you wanted an antique or collectible 20 plus years ago you went to an antique store, flea market, yard sale or an auction. Now you go to your computer. Again, you know this. It's what happened to supply and demand or the economics of the whole thing. The Internet opened your eyes to the word "rare." Here's a great line. It's rarer to be rare now than it was then.

Back then, when you went to an antique store and they had an amazing, "rare" Beatles lunchbox. The Holy Grail in their store. You'd never seen one in real life and they only wanted $1,500 for it. You scratched and saved for that treasure.

Today, you Google Beatles lunchboxes and 15 of them turn up on eBay, one on Etsy, two at online auctions and now you have choices. Not rare in your eyes now. You can be selective about condition. You want the best one, so you don't bid on or buy the dented ones.

There are three you like and you realize they are not hard to find at all. There are several available every week online. You have no sense of urgency as you can wait until you have some money to buy one for maybe $300.

Did I mention that the $1,500 lunchbox in your hometown back 20 plus years could be put on layaway? Ask a Millennial what layaway is.

I still have people bring in their family heirlooms, tell us of their legend and then I spend two seconds on Google in front of them to show them 20 just like them. It's very deflating and I try to brace them for it. It's funny how in many instances they will explain to me the subtle difference of theirs and what makes theirs unique and nothing like the same exact thing I am showing them. Hard to fight an emotionally charged family legend with facts. I try to explain with grace.

Let's get back to the world market and the benefits of new buyers and collectors. I am talking Asia and its rapidly expanding economy. What this means to us is new buyers and new collectors. And boy are they buying.

The first wave of interest in this trend seems to be the "They want their stuff back" phase. I'll get in to specifics, but also try to explain some of the past trends that help us understand what's happening. Perhaps I can forecast what I think is going to be a bright future.

CHINESE ANTIQUE MARKET: A GOLD MINE FOR FOUND TREASURES AT AUCTION

Sold to the highest bidder! Whether it's an estate auction or eBay, it's always exciting to 'win' in an auction bidding frenzy. And for consignors, the hope is that interest in the collectible item is strong. I've seen the ups and downs of what buying and selling at auction truly reveals: fair market value. The thrill of a record-breaking auction can influence demand for a particular artist, a style of jewelry, pop-culture ephemera and more. Likewise, soft prices realized for a particular genre of art, a china set, Hummel figurines and more indicate declining demand based on cyclical trends and the tastes of a younger generation.

What's hot right now? The Chinese antique market continues to be a gold mine for found treasures at auction. A well carved, decorated blanket chest recently sold at our Scottsdale auction house for $10,000. Sold as part of a Scottsdale resident's estate sale, this treasure from the Orient silenced the crowd as online bidders from Asia began to battle live online during a webcast auction. The chest turned out to be made of finely carved and highly prized Zitan wood. Zitan is an extremely dense wood that sinks in water. It is a member of the Rosewood family and the box dated to the Middle Qing Dynasty period. The bidding began at $50 and ended up eclipsing the estate's wildest dreams. What was even more unreal was that the owners told our staff that their father purchased the chest at a local thrift store for $50 just five years ago.

This is a trend we continue to see in the Chinese antique market. As China's burgeoning economy blossoms and its new affluent "middle class" begins to collect history, the world is the new market and Asian collectors are proving to be serious shoppers. Prices on all things oriental have been skyrocketing. It's a trend we have seen for the past five years and it shows no signs of slowing down.

For many Chinese collectors, it's a matter of reclaiming valuable items that were taken from them. During the Cultural Revolution in China, the mere possession of many of these items became outlawed. Often confiscated, these treasures and antiquities made their way to the United States though trade and importation. Every record we see as of late seems to be in this genre.

With each passing year, China becomes more open. Collectors want jade, bronze works, cloisonné, cinnabar, furnishings, and fine decor. Ivory has been the only trend we have seen reversed. As the laws tighten to restrict illegal trade in modern reproductions, it frightens purchasers of even the most antique of items. The uncertainty makes the ivory market volatile, which is completely understood when investing or collecting. But on the upside, if I were to be hunting the estate and yard sale markets today, I would be buying all things oriental. That's where today's lottery ticket money is best spent!

Now let me give you a little mid-20th Century collector's world history to explain my further theory and why I think other forecasts are good. Follow me. China is buying now, as I explained. Its middle class is emerging, has disposable income, and is nostalgic for the past. In the late 1980s and early 1990s, we saw the same trend with the Japanese. Their industrialized booming economy with a generation in their collector phase of life with disposable income made for a great market for sellers and these new buyers couldn't get enough and prices soared. It started with buying their stuff back and moved in to all things collectible. I think the emerging Chinese market as well as the just-starting-to-peak Indian market may do the same exact thing. Collect their history, then start to collect pop culture and the exotic. American and European antiques would be exotic to their culture just as theirs is to ours. Only a theory, but we've seen it happen several times in the collectibles and antiques market.

See how it's just a cycle. After World War II, Americans bought European antiques. In the 50s and 60s, we were booming, while Europe and Asia were selling history at a bargain, and we were buying it all. Then Europe and Asia started to boom in the 80s and 90s, and they bought back what they sold to us and the circle continues. Again, this is not new and has happened throughout world history. It's just that there are now faster cycles with the smaller world the Internet created.

WHAT'S KILLING IT? CONTEMPORARY AND MODERN ART

Trendy is getting quite spendy. I continue to be amazed by contemporary and modern art values. Art post-1950 in that modernist style seems to be unstoppable. Our most recent annual New Year's Day auction featured a few fine examples of modern art by Harry Bertoia, Bernard Buffet and George Rodrigue. I was curious to see what the market would bear at a well-publicized public local auction. You will see pieces like these turn up in the major auction houses all over the world, but with the advent of social media and online marketing these classes of items are showing up more regionally as in this case.

I understand that these artists are not household names like Dali, Picasso and Chagall, but in the art collector's world, they are fairly well known. Harry Bertoia was an Italian-American artist, sculptor and modern furniture designer born in 1915. His sculptures can be found all over the world and many of his furniture designs are still in production today. Our Scottsdale auction house featured a sound sculpture that stood approximately 55 inches tall. It was an odd form constructed of brass and melt-coated copper. Produced in 1956, it created quite a lot of buzz prior to the sale. People flew into town to inspect it and we received many phone calls prior to the sale. The bidding was furious, opening at $50,000 and by the time it was said and done a phone bidder won the piece for $120,000, eclipsing our $70,000 to $90,000 pre-auction estimate.

Then there is George Rodrigue, who is famous for his depictions of the Blue Dog. His prices seem to be on an upward climb since his death in 2013. Cliché as it may be, it's not often true that an artist's death makes the price go up. It's true it happens in certain cases, but it is not as common as people believe. But, back to the Blue Dog. This wonderful piece sold for $42,500, which turned out to be a good investment for the folks who had recently purchased it for $25,000 in the artist's gallery.

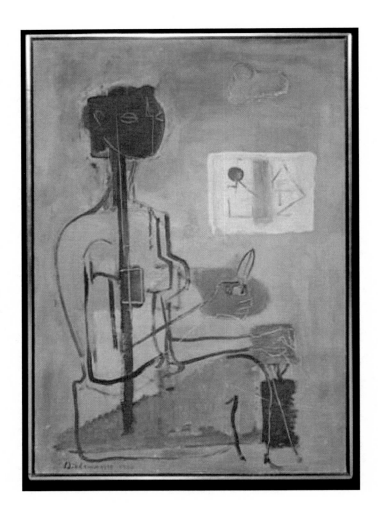

One of the surprises we had was the Bernard Buffet. It was an excellent still life example, featuring a mandolin, fruit and tableware. It was estimated to be worth between $20,000 and $30,000 before the sale and the final bid came in at $57,500. This seems to be the artist's trend for the past few years. Commanding top dollar in its style and genre.

Although I often feel like we, the auctioneers and appraisers, are the messengers who gets shot, I still love the auction world and antique business. It's always an adventure and I hope I have other market busters to report in the future.

GUITARS ROCK AT AUCTION

Did you play a musical instrument as a kid? Well, good news -- the public's love of musical instruments has never waned.

Before I got into the auction business, I played guitar in a rock band and owned a used musical instrument shop. So, I know a lot about this topic. In my 25 plus years of buying and selling vintage guitars, I have not seen the genre in a recession. In fact, it just seems to keep getting better.

The most sought after guitars are actually getting priced out of afford-ability for the average collector. Your 1950s and 60s Gibson Les Paul's, American Fender Stratocasters, Telecasters, Gretsch Falcons and the like are all commanding top dollar on the secondary market. It's nothing for some of these to command $20,000 to $30,000.

Today we are seeing the player collect some of the 1970s and 80s bizarre and retro guitars from the U.S. and Japan as these are still affordable, but continuing to climb in value.

Here's a little back story. I owned and operated my used musical instrument shop for 10 years in the 1990s, and I would often see these guitars. At the time, they were literally selling for under a few hundred dollars. Oh, if I could only jump into a hot tub time machine and tell the young me to hang onto these and also to not date a few of those girls.

Let me give you just a few examples. We would sell a Daphne Blue, a rare color, Fender Jaguar for $150. Today, that's a $6,000 guitar. A 1975 Ibanez Destroyer was $200. We just sold a Van Halen version for $3,750. Mosrite guitars were about $300 and now $2,000. From 1995 to 2015 we have seen an amazing surge. You might have taken guitar lessons on an old Silvertone Electric with a built-in amplifier from Sears that your parents paid $69 for. That's about $500 today. Who knew that would happen? Names like Univox, Teisco Del Ray, Kay, Harmony, Hamer, Charvel and ESP may all sound alien to some of you, but collectors want these guitars.

That example is not just limited to guitars. Many a vintage saxophone, clarinet and flute have seen similar trends. Look in your closet. You may have a hidden treasure you long forgot about from your high school band days. Did you play a Selmer Mark 6 saxophone? That is now about $5,000. Some Ludwig Snare drums are $2,000. A Conn Constellation trumpet is now bringing in about a $1,000 at auction.

Many savvy Millennials are finding ways to make a little extra money, non-Uber style, by yard sailing. I believe looking for musical instruments is a no brainer. Many of our "pickers," no guitar pun intended, bring us these finds on a regular basis. It's a quick turn at the auction for some extra spending money.

I am very passionate about vintage musical instruments as it was my first love in the collecting world. From the trend I see, I am not alone. Music is timeless. I wish I could say that about Hummels and Beanie Babies. No one wants Hummels, Beanie Babies or Herpes. If you haven't noticed I really beat up on Hummels. I am starting to feel guilty, but I'll probably do it three or four more times before I am done with this book. If Hummels were an ice cream flavor it would taste like Avon.

A LUNCHBOX PERFORMS SUPER

At the auction market I must admit, I have always been drawn to toys and collectibles. Who doesn't love seeing a fond piece of their childhood memory? Barbie, G.I. Joe, that Tin Robot, a clapping monkey or even your own personal Poltergeist clown. Okay, maybe you chose to forget that last one. My point is that people just light up at a toy and collectible auction. Recently in Scottsdale, we held a collection that truly represented how this market continues to perform as well as shed more light on its current trends.

What wowed us? It was really the fine collection of lunchboxes. Many sold way beyond their pre-auction estimates. The highlight was a 1954 Superman box that realized $1,200 and was won by an online bidder from New York. All these boxes were sold as part of one Scottsdale resident's personal, life-long collection. A 1962 Dudley Do-Right lunchbox and thermos by the Universal Vacuum Products Company sold for more than $1,000. It was followed by a 1963 Jetsons Dome metal lunchbox made by Aladdin for just under $750. Both were snatched up by a local bidder who I am told is an avid collector himself. I spoke about a Beatles lunchbox as an example earlier in the book, which shows how the market shifts.

But let me explain how trends we see work overall. The price curve is moving on toys and collectibles to what we used to refer to as modern-era toys. The 1930s Lionel and Marklin trains that were once the Holy Grail stalwart of toys have been replaced by the Aurora T-Jet slot car and Hot Wheels Redlines from the 1960s. The old G.I. Joe replaced by Star Wars and Transformers Robots. Shirley Temple by She-Ra. That's the action figure He-Man's girlfriend if I lost you.

Why is this happening? It's simple and seems to have always been true of this genre. As the generation that played with, owned or wanted to have these toys moves into the disposable income period of their lives, they get nostalgic and want to reclaim their childhood. Demand goes up and so does the price. Then, 15 to 20 years later, when they start to sell off their collections, so do others in their generation and they flood the market. So, you see prices of those items go down. I have said a lot of this earlier, but I hope this illustration better delivers the message.

Again, my advice to collectors is to strike while the iron is hot. When you hear crazy prices for what you collect sell, sell, sell. More often than not I hear, "I am going to wait. Prices are still going up." Then back into the paid storage rental unit they go, down go the prices and still they wait. Am I always right? No! Star Wars keeps amazing me. I have been telling people to sell these toy collectibles before the bottom drops out, but they keep performing. When the next new movie comes out, the original 1970s and 80s figures will probably strike again. Or Strike Back! Some things buck this trend, but I have found it to be about 95 percent accurate.

HAVE TRAINS PASSED THEIR STATION?

The iconic toy train set went from being every boy's dream to a collectible. Really, the 1970s saw the demand change, as the train was no longer what every boy had to have. The crazes moved on to slot cars, action figures and then with the 80s, video game systems and so on.

This transition period and change in demand from hot, to collectible, to passé is not surprising.

No one disputes the train as an icon of man's coming of age, the Industrial Revolution and really a game changer. Just as influential it was in changing the world, it changed the toys that boys wanted. Right after World War I, the train became the most popular toy in America. Companies like Lionel and American Flyer became household names. The Germans and most of Western Europe were already ahead of us with companies like Bing and

Marklin being the leaders. From 1930 until the late 60s, the train set was a staple in every home and around just about everyone's Christmas tree.

As the toy's new interest waned, the collector, nostalgic to recapture his childhood and now armed with a disposable income, began to pay record prices for the Pre-War rare sets. As generations grew older and moved into this collectible generation, they purchased the sets of their era. The 1950s and 1960s sets even gained respectability in the collector's eyes. You see, people seem to collect what they had as a child or what they couldn't have or afford. Sometimes they collect just to capture that memory or share it with someone they love.

The end of this collectible phase comes when you have a perfect storm as we do now in the collectibles market. The generation doing the collecting now didn't have train sets growing up. A few might remember their grand-dad's, but the interest is not there. This is coupled with Baby Boomers selling their prized collections and soon we will see the market getting flooded. So, you have limited demand and an abundance of supply. As you recall, these were the most popular toys so a ton of them were made. Over the past five years I have given my clients the advice to sell and sell now, unless you are saving them for a few generations when interest may return, but you and I won't be around to see it.

Slot Cars, Hot Wheels, Star Wars, Legos and the like now have all the interest, as they're what the 1970s and 1980s generations played with. I love the train example and use it often as I feel it best illustrates everything in collectible trends. You can exchange trains with classic cars, vintage radios, Barbie dolls, GI Joes and any other item with an iconic genera-tional appeal. The demand will not last forever and the supply when liqui-dated is great. Most people hold onto their collections too long and while I understand the passion behind the collections, it's important to recognize when the time is right to let go.

HOW HOT ARE HOT WHEELS?

Who would have thought that a 59-cent Mattel Hot Wheels Redline die-cast toy car could be worth thousands of dollars, but today they are quite the craze. Of course it's the rare, promotional or highly sought out versions that command the highest dollars, but just recently this market has really heated up. If you have some late 60s or early 70s Mattel toys that are still in their original packages have someone check them out as the proverbial 'Iron is Hot.'

A great local example came to us by way of a recent appraisal fair. A couple of guys came in with the classic Mattel Hot Wheels car case that all of us boys had when we were kids. Inside was a great little collection of these toy cars. Upon initial inspection, we knew they were quite good and they were still in excellent condition. This collection was well kept and we learned that as boys, they were not allowed to play with these particular cars. Their grandfather was an electrician who did some work at a Mattel factory in California and had acquired the cars before they were thrown away as errors, unpainted and test-painted cars. Thank goodness someone in the family had the foresight to put them away. Here's the tale of the tape. When we sold them at auction the collection realized more than $24,000. Much better than our initial $3,000 to $5,000 estimate for the collection. The unpainted examples stole the show. Meaning that Mattel never painted the cars as errors or blanks. The 1967 Camaro brought $2,750. The Custom VW was the star at $4,250 and the Camaro that was in an unreleased color soared to $3,250. These prices would sound crazy to some folks, but when I tell you the 1969 Prototype Beach Bomb VW Van sold recently for $72,000 you can see these cars are pretty hot. Like new and in the package are commanding amazing prices as well. It's not just the prototypes. Even loose, used cars can fetch hundreds if you have the right colors or right models. Want a few examples to search for? Find a 1971 Purple Olds 442, a 1974 Blue Rodger Dodger, a 1970 Ed Shaver Custom AMX, a 1968 Custom Volkswagen without Sunroof or a 1968 White Enamel Camaro and you should have well over $1,000 in your hand! As usual, contact an expert if you have any questions, as there are color variations, condition issues and the overall market conditions to consider. All this said, I think this market is hot now and might be something you want to consider taking a look at should you be lucky enough to have some or stumble across them at a yard sale!

YOU THINK POKÉMON PLAYERS
ARE CRAZY? THINK AGAIN.

I thought it would be beneficial to enlighten you all on trends, fads and crazes and how it can affect collectors, collections and their resale values. Unless you lived under a rock, Pokémon in 2016 was all the rage... again. What began as a Nintendo Game Boy video game in the mid-1990s has blown up into a franchise that now includes video games, trading card games, animated television shows, movies, comic books and toys. The 2016 RPG, or online role playing game, had caused a small surge as if almost overnight, but the Pokémon craze and underground collectors have never really gone away -- they were just lying in wait, like a Pokémon!

Some of the original collector's card sets from 1999 can realize a few thousand dollars on eBay and some of the rare cards can bring several thousand dollars each. The recent craze can even cause a spike, especially with the new players causing new demand from more players. The other items and collectibles from the franchise are seen as cool, hip and very retro, and therefore, hot with the collectors.

The Pokémon craze is not an anomaly. In toys and games, examples include versions based on Star Wars, Transformers, Mario Brothers, GI Joe, and Teenage Mutant Ninja Turtles. They become known as franchises, developers and creators capitalize on everything to do with them. I want to be clear -- fads can cause people to collect anything and everything and if the franchise doesn't survive a generation, they tend to be just that, a fad. A huge collection with no interest. Think Beanie Babies, Cabbage Patch Kids and Pogs. All equally as hot as Pokémon and Star Wars in their heyday, but now seem like a distant memory and as collectibles, nearly worthless.

Now, let me tell you about the ones you probably don't know. The cult-like following games that have never gone away, just underground. But to their collectors, they are highly prized and more valuable than their household named friends. Do you remember Magic: The Gathering? The role playing card game that's underground now, but whose cards can sell for thousands and even tens of thousands for rare variants. I wouldn't be surprised if their developer is not seeing this Pokémon craze and looking to come back with a vengeance. The father of all these types of games, Dungeon and Dragons, is still out there as well. They have highly prized collectibles that you probably never heard of. We just sold a few loose D&D toys for $110 that most people would have put out for the yard sale at $5.

With these examples, I'm just scratching the surface of what's lurking out there, like a rare Pokémon.

I talk a lot about toys and you'd think I was a collector or a big kid. Okay, the latter is true. I just think they illustrate the collector's mindset best, but it really relates to all things. Let's delve into other areas of interest, shall we?

WHAT'S DOING WELL? STYLISH VINTAGE WATCHES

Lately, there's been a lot of buzz about smartwatches. Many of these come with accelerometers, heart rate monitors, GPS and some even have the capacity to make phone calls. Pretty cool yes, but not as distinctive and stylish as a vintage watch in my opinion.

Some collectors fascinated with horology will pay top dollar for vintage timepieces, pocket watches and wristwatches. Whether it's for the sophistication and pedigree that comes with a vintage dress watch or the cool factor of a dive watch from the 1960s or 70s. All in all, vintage watches in general are doing well at auction.

The most famous of recent auction history was the Patek Philippe Supercomplication pocket watch that fetched $24 million in 2014 at a Sotheby's auction in Switzerland. Dating back to the early 1930s, the watch took several years to build and featured 24 "complications" or functions.

Patek Philippe and rare Rolex watches do very well at auction. Recently, during our annual New Year's Day auction we sold a custom Rolex 18-karat Presidential Men's Diamond Watch for $22,000. Dating back to the mid-1980s, it was a true showstopper featuring diamonds, rubies, a fire opal face and a diamond-encrusted band and bezel.

Other classic brands that I see doing well at auction include Breitling, Movado, Jaeger-LeCoultre, Heuer Autavia, Omega, Racine, Tudor, Mido, and IWC (International Watch Company) among others.

What to look for if you're bidding on a vintage watch? As always, do your research about the brand and understand the mechanics of the watch. Examine the condition in person if you can or have a friend do it for you. If the watch is missing parts research how easy it is to find replacement parts. The last thing you want to do is spend more money repairing the watch than you paid for it.

Ask to see provenance and try to find out if the previous owners specialized in collecting the brand you want to purchase. Some collectors like to own a variety of different watches, while others will spend a lifetime collecting one or two brands. These collectors really know their stuff and have made discerning purchases.

Finally, be wary of fake luxury watches. Check typefaces and engravings to make sure they are authentic. Listen to the watch – if the ticking is really loud, that's a red flag. Weigh it – often fake watches are lighter since they are made with less expensive materials. If you're unsure, have a professional assess it.

Like anything vintage, you will likely come across watches that have dials and other parts that have been replaced or refinished. These watches will be less desirable to serious collectors who are always on the hunt for original dials and unpolished original cases.

Again, nothing against smartwatches, but besides style another thing a vintage watch has going for it is that it can't get hacked!

I talk about toys and musical instruments most passionately, but I also have a fondness for vintage electronics. I find this to be a little-known collectible, subculture and something you or Boomer parents might have that you might not realize is super cool to the urban, hipster millennial.

ARE YOU A DIAGNOSED AUDIOPHILE?

Are you an audiophile or do you know one? Many people have this affliction and don't even know it. An audiophile is a person with a love for – okay
-- an obsession with the high-quality playback of music. Why do I bring
this subject up? The audiophile's addiction to sound commands them to
collect vintage sound equipment. To these connoisseurs of sound, nothing
can replace the audio characteristics of many of these past technologies.

The tube amp is a great example. The warm sounds of an old vac-
uum tube power amp cannot be matched by today's digital amplifiers.
Many high-end boutique manufacturers are out there, ready to take your
arm and leg, as they promise to build you a custom piece with this old
tech. However, many of these great old pieces that are in high demand

are in storage units, garages, thrift stores and maybe your closet. It's an underground market almost, as I see most of America has no clue to its cult-like following.

Brands like McIntosh, Scott, Technics, Sansui, Fisher, Marantz and Audio Research are just a few examples of these old manufacturers. All of this is just the tip of the iceberg when it comes to this genre of collectors. They are just as fanatical about turntables (record players), guitar amps, sound effect pedals and don't let me get started on old speakers.

My hope is to put you "in the know" before you have a yard sale and put out your old clunker stereo thinking it's outdated and worthless and mind you, it may be. Many are not collectible and are considered to make better door stops or boat anchors, but always check first. Most appraisers, auctioneers and vintage record shops can find out if you have a hidden gem.

To best illustrate this phenomenon, we recently sold a McIntosh MC2205 for $950 at auction that the owners had slated for the dumpster. An old pair of Lansing speakers, very unassuming, realized $750 at one of our auctions last summer. Again, the movers were surprised when I didn't send them in for donation. In my research, I just came across an old Kenwood turntable that sold for $4,250 at auction just a few weeks ago. Yes, that's $4,000 for a record player!

It gets crazier. An old Western Electric tube record player preamplifier just sold on eBay for $22,000. To the layman, that's the thingy you put between your record player and your power amplifier. That must really make everything sound better! This is pre-remote control, people. Actually, I must admit I do get it. I have heard these serious collector's sound systems and there is a huge difference. It's not just nostalgia for the old, but it does sound better and they can back it up with scientific evidence. But in today's world of convenience, we just pop in our ear buds and enjoy our inferior music reproduction.

Here's a smooth transition for you...

IS NATIVE AMERICAN JEWELRY COMING BACK IN STYLE?

Does my writing give you whiplash? Imagine being in my ADD brain. If this line is still here my editor either likes my sense of humor or quit.

In the auction world, we follow trends closely. Keeping current with what's hot and what's not is becoming a science. These trends seemed to have a longer shelf life you could count on, but with each passing year as attention spans get shorter we must stay on top of things. It's really so we can manage a seller's expectations and potential resale of the things we bring to market for our consignors.

A trend I have noticed of late is the return of value regarding Native American jewelry and I mean the "good stuff." Squash blossom necklaces, silversmith artisan cuff bracelets, mid-century inspired Zuni and Navajo rings and the list goes on. You need to know your makers and their hallmarks, which is where an expert comes in. Although with a little digging online, a savvy "Googler" can find references to these hallmarks and do a little sleuthing on their own. The artist's name, as in just about all things, is paramount to value.

A simple, unassuming silver bracelet valued at about $20 by your local pawn shop can be worth several thousand dollars if it's by Charles Loloma. A Hopi silver and turquoise tufa-cast bracelet by Charles Loloma just sold in Chicago for $10,000. The silver value was about $50. We just had a wonderful auction surprise as a Fred Peshlakai bracelet soared to $6,500. I believe this to be the record-setting price at auction for one of his pieces. This is a great trend to see here in the desert Southwest as we have a lot of fine works in the Valley.

This past auction really made me take a look back at the trend and study our auction analytics. I really do see prices on the increase for these hand-crafted works of art. Post-recession, the prices have been on the rise. This is contrary to the price of silver which spiked in 2011 almost reaching $50 and has since come down to earth hovering around $15. For the last few years, it's been more about the workmanship and less about the silver content. Imagine that! Art over substance.

It's been a silent trend. I don't hear too many people talking about it. It's rare to see a market when it's good to sell and may also be a sound investment at the same time. I think it may be the mid-century design of many of these pieces, also in vogue in furniture and current tastes. Or it's the simple design and hand-craftsmanship of many of the pieces. Whatever it is, I just thought you might find it a bit interesting especially if you or a loved one owns Native American jewelry.

This whole Native American Jewelry thought process sent me down another wormhole of thought.

WILL OUR WESTERN ROMANCE SURVIVE?

I often look for trends and try to forecast what we see coming in the auction world. Being here in the desert Southwest, one of the most common genres we sell is Western art and collectibles. I'm often asked about the best timing to sell these collections. After more than 20 years of handling many large estates at auction I am starting to see a trend that tells me now is the time. When meeting with families and seeing this generational shift in tastes and collection, my fear is that the Millennial is not going to be collecting this genre. I worry that its effects will be felt until the romance returns some generation later or as the forthcoming generations fall in love again. This is why I say that now is the time to sell instead of waiting to be caught in the downward spiral of prices as we've seen too many times with other collectibles.

My parents waited too long regarding antiques and primitives. We saw the late 80s boom of Colonial furniture and folk art as my parents collected and then when it was time to sell the market had shifted and it was too late. Selling for pennies on the dollar or a tenth of what they had paid.

Will the prices come back? Yes. Will we live long enough to see it? I don't know. I am not a fatalist as I see it's just a 40-year or so cycle in most all things. However, like most, I am not storing things for 40 years for their maturity. Back to Western art and collectibles, the signs are here and I'd be a seller now. Western listed artists are selling well. Bronze works, oil paintings and all things rustic are still commanding prices, but the buyer still tends to be the Boomer. And how long will they be buyers versus sellers?

Recently we had a Dave McGary "Last Stand Hill" bronze that realized $24,000 with buyer's premium. It was a beautiful depiction of Sioux warriors and there was a lot of demand, but I wondered what a Millennial would pay for it five years from now. Millennials tend to be minimalists. I wonder if the "namers" of the generations saw that coming. A Frank McCarthy, famous for his western pulp illustrations, original oil on board hammered for $8,500 and I have the same feeling that three to four years from now, the buyer pool may be greatly diminished.

Simple supply and demand. One hope and perhaps a silver lining, is that we've become a world economy and as more live auctions are broadcast internationally online, other cultures may have an interest in collecting our heritage. This has happened before and may happen again. Pop culture, movies and the media can greatly influence this. Shows like HBO's Westworld can influence buyers and peak interest. After all, Game of Thrones has me wanting to buy a throne.

I am sure you have noticed, I like to throw in tips at certain points for my pickers, my sellers and my buyers. I like to keep the playing field level and just let you know what I see going on in my world, which really is the auction world and secondary market. Now, onto another topic that is of interest to all generations whether you're a Boomer, Gen X'er or a Millennial.

5 THINGS TO KNOW WHEN SELLING YOUR FAMILY'S SILVER AND GOLD

Be it your father's coin collection, your mother's estate jewelry, or your grandparent's silverware, when it comes to selling silver and gold a little knowledge and a basic understanding of the market can go a long way.

1. **Find out today's spot price.** The spot price is what the particular metal is trading for in ounces. This information can easily be found on the Internet or the market section of the newspaper.

2. **Find out how much metal you have in ounces.** A basic postal scale will assist you.

3. **Know what percentage of the metal is in there.** A little algebra here, but I'll walk you through it. Sterling is .925, meaning it has a content of 92.5 percent of silver. 14K gold is .585 or 58.5 percent gold. 18K gold is .750 or 75 percent gold. Example: You have a set of sterling silver spoons that weigh 20 ounces. So, as I write this today, the spot price is $15.95 per ounce. So, 20 ounces times $15.95 equals 319. Times that by .925 and you have $295.07 of silver value.

4. **Getting Appraisals.** Now you are armed with some knowledge as you head to the nearest, "We Buy Gold & Silver" place and you ask, "How much?" They come back with $150 and you are shocked and appalled. Don't be. Here's the fourth thing you need to know: They are in business to make money. Don't be mad... shop around. If you ask three different people, you will most likely get three different prices and that is fine.

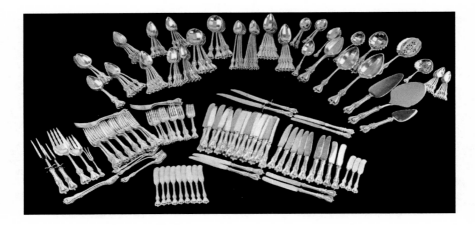

5. **A name can be everything.** Is your silver or jewelry Tiffany, Cartier, Buccellati, Russian or even a rare pattern? These can significantly add to value and you can bet no one is going to tell you that. I find auctioning these items will allow the fair market to decide that potential added value. A set of Buccellati spoons weighing about 20 ounces just sold at our auction house for $2,000.

I don't want to forget about coins. For the most part, their particular silver or gold content is the value and several coins have different percentages of their particular base metal. However, just like a brand name can add value to silver and jewelry a mint mark or rarity can increase value. Known as a key date to coin collectors, some of these can be worth several hundreds or even thousands of dollars. A common Morgan silver dollar is worth about an ounce of silver, so about $16. But, if your Morgan silver dollar has a Carson City mint mark, it could bring $100 on up.

I am going to hide from several business associates who are not going to like this information, but if I save you from giving away the golden or silver goose, I can sleep much better at night.

IS YOUR $20 BILL WORTH $20,000?

I thought it would be interesting to talk about the value of currency, especially with all of the recent news from the Treasury Department about changing the $20, $10 and $5 bills to include Harriet Tubman and other women and civil rights leaders over the next decade.

Don't tune out -- this is not a boring inflation, economic story, I promise. It's about the value of old bills that may be lying around. I am talking about old Federal Reserve Notes, silver certificates, "Large Notes," which were some 40 percent larger than bills of today, postage currency, military certificates and the like. I have run into people who believe that because these are out of circulation they're nearly worthless or just a conversation piece. Much to the contrary and in many cases, this market has been heating up.

In the past, paper currency did not have the interest of the coin collectors. The demand and value was not there, but I believe logic kicked in to the collector.

What's the logic? The rarity, as paper did not survive like coins had. Limited circulation and condition always meant the most to the coin collector. Paper has this, hands down. Paper has more enemies than metal.

What if I told you a $20 bill from 1861 could be worth more than $500,000? It's true. In fact, in September 2015 a fine example sold for $675,000 at an auction in Texas. For a better earthly example a $10 bill from 1914 just sold in Illinois for $550. That's really what I'm trying to express to you. You may have an old $5 bill in your wallet and not realize it's worth $250. Another example I love is old, large denominations that are out of circulation. $500 bills regularly sell for more than $1,000 and $1,000 bills can fetch $2,000 or more.

Other things to look for are errors. Anything significant on a bill that occurred during the printing process can drive up the value to a certain set of collectors. If you think you have a bill with an error, make sure you contact an expert to authenticate it. One 1988 $5 bill with a seal error just sold at auction for $390.

There is a lot to cover regarding paper currency collecting and values and far too much for this book, but I hope I set you on the path of taking another look at the change you received at Starbucks. I personally collect my odd change finds and last year, I turned $38 in $110, with some $2 and $1 bills. Not retiring, but a little bit of fun and a great dinner somewhere.

OTHER GENRES OF NOTE....

Tuning In To The Value Of Music Boxes

Nothing captures a child or an adult for that matter like a beautiful mechanical music box. I love when we have one in the gallery and it's fired up. You'll see everyone stop for a second and take it in. They have always seemed to have that effect on people. I can remember vividly the first music box I ever saw. It was my sister's ballerina jewelry box that played the theme from Love Story. Just typing that has ear wormed the tune back into my brain.

The history of the music box dates back to the ninth century when Persian brothers invented a hydro-powered organ with interchange-able cylinders. Europe began to see early music boxes appear in the 13th century. The classic pinned barrel of the music box as we know it came to light in approximately 1598 and they're still made today. The majestic and golden era of the music box took place during the 18th and 19th centuries. The French and Swiss were making works of art with fine woods, elaborate mechanical movements and all the bells and whis-tles. Literally, many had bells, drums and whistles. Only the most affluent in this period could afford such a thing.

In the late 19th century, the metal disc players began to overtake the cylinder based systems and became affordable. Then came the player piano, gramophone and the record player, which kind of made the music box passé. As with all trends of out with the old, in with the new, the music box got lost for a bit. However, now prized by collectors and truly appreciated for their ingenuity, elaborate mechanics and beckoning a time long by these little masterpieces can command great prices at auction. At our Scottsdale auction house a rare, coin-operated Capital Penny Arcade music box by F. G. Otto & Sons sold for $7,800 in 2012. Two years later a beautiful Regina Model 35 upright bow front automatic12-disc changer circa 1899-1910 realized $15,600 in our New Year's Day auction. More recently, a Regina Music Box Company music box sold at our auction for $1,920 in October 2015.

These are just a few examples of local finds, but an international search of auction results shows that certain rare models can fetch in the hundreds of thousands of dollars. An auction in Indiana sold a Hupfeld Super Pan Model III Pan Orchestra for $495,000 in February of 2012. I really believe the music box has staying power in the antique and collectible world for many reasons. Clock and mechanical works have always fascinated man, music has always been at our core and they always seem to remind us of our childhood in some way.

What's The Worth Of Your Vintage Camera?

It appears that Paul Simon's 1973 lyrics, "Mama, don't take my Kodachrome away" from his hit song, *Kodachrome*, may have new life despite the fact that Kodak officially retired the color film in 2009 to make way for the digital revolution.

If you're too young to know what I'm talking about you missed out on a great era...it was a time when cameras were considered to be like status symbols. If Nikon, Canon, and Olympus were Cadillacs, precision cameras like Hasselblad and Leica were in an elite class like Lamborghinis and Ferraris.

Passionate photographers stood behind their brands and would debate which was better. It wasn't that much different from what was happening with audio. As a former musician, I used to demand the best quality receivers, speakers and sound systems. Same thing for photographers, only it was all about the optics.

Back then, once you committed to a brand you were stuck because all of the manufacturer mounts were different. Some of you may be able to relate to buying three bodies, five lenses and yet another new lens would come out six months later and there you were sacrificing whatever you had in order to pay for it.

Fast forward to the mid-1990s when a lot of photographers saw how technology was changing. Some – and many to this day – frowned upon the idea of a digital camera. Many of the purists and hobbyists gave it up and the cameras, lenses, tripods, light tables and other gear got stored away.

Today, many of these vintage cameras are hitting the secondary market. Recently, we had bidders fighting over a Leica M3-977 camera and Perrin case that went for $1,295.40 with buyer's premium. I think this one would have done much better had there not been a small crack on the grips.

The hammer price on a Hasselblad 500C medium format SLR camera at that same auction was $550. Still quite collectible and a good buy for the lucky collector who won the bid. They regularly sell on eBay in the $800 to $1,000 range.

At another recent auction, the hammer price was $550 for a Nikon AS camera outfit with all its accessories and case. Granted, the consignor probably spent significantly more on this and other photographic equipment during that time, but selling it now for a few hundred dollars is better than letting it sit in a closet collecting dust.

I'm always fascinated when we see these old cameras come into the auction house. From the 19th century wood cameras and box cameras to rangefinders, 35 mm, Polaroids and more, these treasures from our past were instrumental in capturing the story of our lives. Whether people are collecting them now for décor or other reasons, it's nice to see a renewed interest and respect for them.

Some Pens Command Powerful Prices At Auction

Recently, we had new pens created with our company logo – a real collectible, I'd like to think.

Okay I'm kidding, but when it comes to selling vintage and luxury pens at auction that's no laughing matter. People will pay top dollar for a writing instrument covered with 18-karat gold, diamonds, rubies and other rare gems. By top dollar I'm talking $40,000 and up for the most luxurious pens in the world. The Aurora Diamante Fountain Pen is considered to be the most expensive pen in the world at $1,470,600. Covered with 30,000 diamonds there is only one in the world and yes I'd love to sell it.

Similar to inkwells, pens have an important place in writing history. Lewis Edson Waterman gets credit for taking the fountain pen to a new level. In 1888, he created very thin grooves in the nib that allowed air to circulate to the ink reservoir, creating a steady flow of ink. In the 1920s, pen manufacturers started to develop plastic pens and by the 1940s ballpoint pens were all the rage.

We're seeing more high-end pens coming through our auction house probably because Baby Boomers and older generations are downsizing or liquidating their estates. Certain brands are expected to do well such as Waterman, Parkers, Wahl-Eversharp and Mont Blanc.

At a recent auction we sold a 14-karat gold Mont Blanc Meisterstück 146 Fountain pen for $240 with buyer's premium. I think we got a fair price for it especially because of its condition. If it was mint we would expect over $600, but due to cosmetic issues and a need for restoration the price was excellent.

In 2014, we auctioned a three-piece Waterman Hundred Year pen and pencil set along with many other collectible pens and pencils. At $900 including buyer's premium, the bidder won a very desirable set that will most likely increase in value, particularly since the Hundred Year pen was the world's first Lucite pen.

Me? I still appreciate the craftsmanship behind a fine pen. I don't need the case to be jewel-encrusted but I do want the ink to flow easily on paper, making a strong statement. Whether I'm closing a deal or signing checks having a quality, vintage pen somehow elevates the experience.

Sure, you could pay retail prices for a new pen. But with so many antique and vintage pens hitting the secondary market right now – if you've done your homework about provenance and examined a pen's condition -- you really can't go wrong with buying a pen at auction.

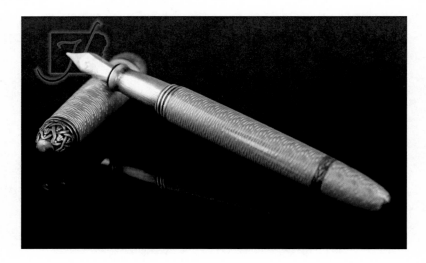

If that doesn't work, stop by the auction house for a free J. Levine pen. I like to think it's sleek and worth something to somebody.

Less Mighty But Let's Discuss

What is it about the sword? These fascinating weapons have been popular at auctions for hundreds of years. Antique, historic, even modern works of art can fetch thousands at auction. Many times it's their personal history, the weapon's rarity or just the design. The Japanese Katana or Samurai Sword have always had an air of mystery. The Spanish Rapier conjures up the Three Musketeers. The Saber brings to mind charging into battle.

Swords of historical significance have crossed the auction block before and have sold for staggering amounts. The Confederate Presentation Sword to General Christopher H. Mott realized more than $300,000 at an auction in 2008. Major General John E. Wool's sword sold for $575,000. The 1812 Presentation Sword of General Winfield Scott brought $1.7 million at the same auction in 2008. So, you can see, the swords can mean serious business both as a weapon and as an auction draw.

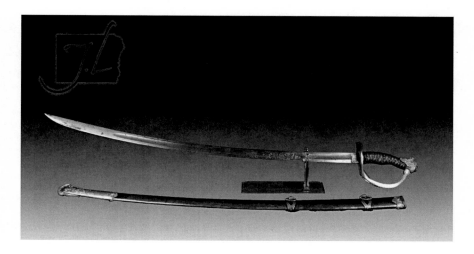

Over the years I've auctioned all types of swords, daggers and knives and I think there will always be a fascination with historic swords, especially since there were less of them made than revolvers. Here are some tips if you're new to collecting.

1. **Know the difference between decorative and functional swords**. Decorative swords were often made with stainless steel that can easily fracture or break under high impact. Functional swords were made with a variety of different steels including Damascus and folded steel. Most functional swords weigh between two and four pounds and were designed to flex and bend.

2. **Research the era in which the sword was produced.** As with any collectible, there are many reproductions on the market and even some original swords that have been restored in some way. Check out Old Swords, MyArmory.com and other resource sites.

3. **Examine markings and rust stains.** Markings can range from country of origin, maker's marks, inspector stamps, arsenal marks and more. Sometimes the lack of a date or mark can help authenticate it. If there is blood on a sword any contact with water will make it bleed red even after thousands of years whereas regular rust will turn brown.

As for what to budget some of the more modern swords are reasonable. In May 2015 we auctioned a 20th century Japanese Samurai Wakizashi sword that realized $1,320. In 2014, we sold an Ikkansai Kasama Shigetsugu tanto or short sword, that sold to an Internet bidder for $3,250.

Once you start collecting swords you'll probably find yourself hooked, especially if you're lucky enough to find a rare one.

The Lure Of The Inkwell

Back to the world of writing, recently we sold a collection of more than 200 exquisite inkwells from one local consignor's collection. She started collecting in the late 1970s purchasing each one from antique shops... never on the Internet.

For you young readers, here's a little history: Back in 1836, ready-made ink was made available and inkwells were created to hold ink. People would take their feather quill or later, metal nib pens, dip it in the inkwell and write.

Many inkwells were portable, but the decorative ones for desks gained popularity quickly. Think of your cell phone case...you have lots of options for designs and materials. Back then, you'd see all types of designs for ink-wells created in cut glass crystal, milk glass, enameled champlevé, brass, bronze, faience pottery, sterling, silver-plate, porcelain, and more.

Clearly, the lure of the inkwell is much more than its decorative style. Before the advent of the fountain pen in the late 19th century these were part of everyone's lives and helped to record everything from national declarations, business deals, literature, love letters and other correspondence. Imagine if rather than tweets today's politicians had to trade insults using a feather quill and an inkwell!

Our consignor's inkwells were made during the "golden age" from 1870 to the 1920s. Her collection included well-known brand names such as Meissen, Limoges, Baccarat, Tiffany, Loetz, Nippon, Dresden, KPM,

Heintz, Gouda pottery, Staffordshire pottery and many others. The star of the auction was a circa 1904 sterling Tiffany desk inkwell which sold for $840 with buyer's premium. I was not surprised as Tiffany usually commands the best prices. Another inkwell that performed well in the auction was a Loetz threaded iridescent glass shell inkwell that sold for $660 with buyer's premium. I think the appeal for this piece was its stunning finish.

One thing to keep in mind about inkwells: like anything else style and condition will affect value, but just because an inkwell was made in the late 1800s doesn't mean it holds more value than one made in the 1940s. Yes, I'm talking about supply and demand. There were considerably less inkwells being produced in the 1940s and brands like Heintz and other "end of Deco" examples from that era continue to realize strong prices at auction.

Of course, technology gave way to the fountain pen and later the ballpoint pen, which probably still seem ancient to some of you reading this. But, I'm seeing a resurgence of interest in many of these vintage pens. Until then, happy writing...whether you're using your tablet, a pen or a Sharpie.

I Won't Pull The Rug Out From Under You

Recently we had a bidding war going on for a true masterpiece. But it wasn't a painting, sculpture or other piece of fine art. It was a signed Iranian silk hunting scene rug that sold for $3,000. This beautiful rug measuring approximately 86" by 52" belonged to a consignor who had traveled the world.

In my two decades of working as an auctioneer, I have seen people pay premium prices for Oriental, Persian, Native American, Pakistani, Turkish, Indian and other types of rugs. Well-made wool and silk rugs from the coast of the Marmara Sea in Hereke command high prices as do the Tabriz of northwest Persia.

If you're in the market for rugs as an investment look for rugs that have proven auction records at the major auction houses. Also, don't be put off by rugs that look faded. Often Oriental rugs for example, have what is called abrash which is a natural change of color over time.

Of course, we always recommend previewing rugs before you bid on them. Look at the back to see how many knots there are per square inch. Ask about the weight to make sure you're not buying a synthetic fiber or flat weave rug. Ask to see the provenance or any documented history about the rug's origin and past ownership.

What rugs are doing well at auction right now? Here are three that have been performing well consistently at our auction house:

Fereghan carpets of Central Persia, a mainstay of designers for years, have always been popular with the European and American markets.

The Agra from India has seen an uptick in demand. They had a major resurgence in popularity in the 1990s and it seems to be happening again.

The Central Persian Isfahan rugs are of great artistic merit and popular with connoisseurs around the globe.

I'm always fascinated when an old tribal or antique rug comes into our auction house. Not only am I enthralled with the craftsmanship that went into creating the rug, but I wonder about the many lives and stories associated with the rug. Yes a rug can finish a room, as a designer may tell you, but I think some of the older rugs can really add an element of mystery and intrigue to a home that a mass-produced rug will never do.

Is Your Purse A Good Investment?

What a strange question, you may think. But no…it's really not. There are so many things that one buys without ever thinking they are a good investment. Most often, they're not. But don't think your purse, clutch or handbag is worthless. I am here to tell you, this might be the best investment of the bunch. Okay, husbands, shoot the messenger now.

Fact: most gallery art you purchase is worth about 20 percent when you walk out the door. For jewelry from a major retailer – it's the same thing. The list goes on, but we see a strange trend in designer handbags and the like. The good ones can hold most of their value especially in relation to the "good investments." Better yet, it's something our clients rarely see any value in and then are surprised to learn.

I can't tell you how many times a client has said, "I donated all my mom's clothing and handbags" and mom was a shopper. This makes me sad and crazy at the same time. The values of some of these vintage purses at auction may surprise you. In fact, in June 2015 Christie's in Hong Kong set a record when it sold a crocodile Hermès Birkin bag for $221,846.

Fashion is big business at auction, and lately I see more excitement over a vintage purse and designer accessories than I do for fine art. Collectors get very serious about a slightly used, upscale brand-named bag that is in good condition. It's a phenomenon that is worldwide. In its May 2015 issue, Glamour Magazine reported that a pair of shoes sells every two seconds on eBay and a purse every five seconds. On mobile the numbers are seven and 11 seconds respectively.

Over the years I've seen near-new designer purses and bags do very well at auction. A Chanel East West white leather quilted handbag realized $550 in 2014 as did a Judith Leiber triangular rhinestone clutch purse. My favorite surprise was a Scottsdale native's used orange Birkin bag that brought in $3,000. The best part was the consignor's astonishment that we were even interested in auctioning it. It was a gift to her and she never even took it out in public. It was headed to the local thrift store.

There are many things like this in your home. These are the items that people believe to have little or no value because they are "used." Yet most feel their art, antiques or collectibles have done nothing but appreciate with age. Supply and demand always reigns supreme and for some reason unbeknownst to this man a good designer purse has demand and therefore value. The short moral to this story is do not donate anything until you contact a professional appraiser. You may be donating an orange Birkin or a Marc Jacobs Carolyn bag that could be worth hundreds or even thousands of dollars.

It's All In A Name

When it comes to art, fine jewelry, furnishing and décor, it's all in a name. Be it your iconic brands like Tiffany and Cartier in jewelry, Picasso and Dali in art, or Herman Miller and Theodore Alexander in furnishings, they all have one thing in common: they are "the money." At auction or on the secondary market these items can still command the value, as they are the names people think of when they think of luxury, expensive and high-quality items.

When you really delve into the secondary market, the hidden gems are the high-end names that are not household names. When inspecting fine, high-end looking items I always look for a name. If it's not signed I ask, "Where did you get this? Do you remember the maker?" Privately, I used to say to myself of course, if I haven't heard of it, it's most likely I just didn't know anyone that could afford it.

The first time I ran into Mario Buccellati jewelry, I was helping with an estate sale in Sedona and saw a beautiful aquamarine ring. When I inspected it with the loop I saw the name Buccellati. I had never heard of it, but when I did a little homework my jaw hit the floor. I saw similar rings for $75,000 and the like. Several of the other pieces were also by the same designer. I quickly became an expert. It's funny, but it's how we all learn this business.

A Prescott home with Le Corbusier chairs had a similar effect on me. They were odd and mid-mod looking, but so is some IKEA furniture. After finding their tags and a little research we determined them to be approximately $6,000 each. I have since found several of them in the Valley.

Don't even get me started on works of art. No one can know, let alone remember all of the listed artists with six-figure auction records. It's amazing how many artists there are that can be of significant value. Does the name James Ensor mean anything to you? It didn't mean a thing to me either. A wonderful woman came by with a little group of prints a few years ago and I said I would be happy to have a look. She just wanted to make sure before she donated them to Good Will. It turned out she had a little gem. It was a nine-by-five inch "sleeper" that realized $1,800 in our Summer Catalog Auction in July 2015.

I was just as surprised as she was. In fact, Ensor has some large prints that can be valued as high as $100,000. A name to those "in the know," but to those who may have them in the garage it is a future thrift store find. To me, it's all in a name.

Who Are You Going To Vote, I Mean, Bid For?

This past presidential election had me thinking. No, not about moving to Sweden, but about Political Memorabilia. It's such an 'easy' collectible and has always been big with collectors. I say easy because it's generally free. The politicians, for the most part, will happily give it to you. Political signs, pinbacks and other ephemera have been around since George Washington and collectors have been scooping them up and collecting ever since.

JFK, Lincoln, Reagan and the Roosevelts have been popular for years. Some of the most desirable pieces are from the modern era. Remember, it does not have to be old to be collectible. Nixon collectors are really coming out of the woodwork recently. Prices have been on the rise. Just as with other collections the desirability or demand is moving the needle.

Some of the earliest political figures even though much older and more rare are not worth the value of more, in demand offerings. It's a common trend nowadays in collectibles. Demand is out-powering supply. The Millennial has heard of Lincoln, but not Buchanan, Kennedy and not Harding.

So, what do you collect now? You collect 'what you know' and not what you don't or just because it's rare. It's just a trend right now I believe, but it's the current truth.

I remember just a few years back watching an original, full size 1980 "America, Reagan Country" presidential campaign poster sell at auction for more than $3,000. In 2015, our auction house sold a few Richard Nixon letters for $16,000 and a Karsh photographic portrait of John. F. Kennedy for $550. That same year, we also sold a White House photograph with seven presidential prints and seven presidential signatures including Bill Clinton, George H. W. Bush, Ronald Reagan, Richard Nixon, Jimmy Carter, Gerald R. Ford, and George W. Bush. That brought in $3,750 at auction.

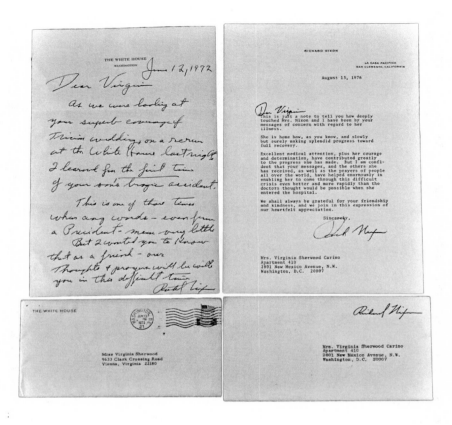

Then there was the time an excellent Franklin D. Roosevelt (FDR) 'Row of Democrats' pinback realized $1,600 at auction. This rare Arizona pin depicted FDR, his vice-presidential candidate Henry Wallace and four-time Arizona governor Sidney P. Osborn, who died in office in 1948 of Lou Gehrig's disease.

Often, these are things we throw away when tasked with cleaning out the estate of a loved one. Thank you letters for political donations can be worth hundreds if not thousands when signed by the right politician. Did your parents donate money to the Eisenhower campaign? He may have sent a signed thank you note! Never overlook those papers your parents kept, unless they are publisher's clearing house notices.

So, what are you going to collect during the next political election cycle? Other than broken TV remotes. I am going to hedge my bets and get the Donald Chia Pet. Yes, that is really a thing you can buy -- you are not watching SNL.

Shoot Me Now

There are two subjects I have avoided really delving into as I have been shot several times. Figuratively of course, but I still have a little PTSD from a few encounters. What subjects you ask? Art and Furniture. I will begin with the "brown sadness" that is antique furniture. I will start with the sad state of affairs, then give some good news and a little education.

I remember the first time an auctioneer said to me, "we don't accept brown furniture." Then a few months later, another auctioneer said, "brown furniture is not selling." Then finally a third person, an antique dealer, told me, "I can't give away brown furniture." Okay this must be a thing, so I asked like an idiot, what's brown furniture? Isn't most furniture brown? Then the light bulb went off. Yes you dummy, they mean most furniture. Sleek, modern, black and white mid-mod and contemporary was and is still hot... brown is not.

They were not being funny either, mind you. They were sad and serious. As soon as someone shows me their grandmother's 1930s depression-era dining room set and asks, "What's this worth?" I want to run out and get a bulletproof vest or just press rewind on my life VCR and not walk in the room. Then I muster up the courage, "$100 to $200" I say. They are confused. Do I mean per chair? Then I really want out. I say, "The whole set. Eight chairs, two leaves and the table." They still don't hear me. I've been asked to leave, been called a con man, stupid and I was even threatened once. "If you don't leave now, I am calling the police." Just for saying what was going to happen at auction.

I have since sold the same sets for $10, $20, $50, $100... you name it. No one is happy here. It's easy to figure out. Large supply and no demand, at all. Used furniture has been pronounced dead by many an antique dealer. I do see it swinging back a little with the repurpose movement, shabby chic and nostalgia. Not to the days of yore, meaning the 1980s and early 90s, but better than a few years ago.

Cyclical Furniture Trends: What's In Demand

Trends come and go in cycles and furniture is no exception. Recently we've been seeing a resurgence of 18th and 19th century furniture...again. In my 20 years of auctioneering, I've seen this period of furniture repeated and reproduced several times over. It seems like bidders can't get enough of mid-modern furniture, but here are a few other manufacturers and styles that are doing well:

Chippendale. Back in the third quarter of the 18th Century cabinet-maker Thomas Chippendale was probably the most famous designer of the time with three distinct designs: Gothic, Rococo and Chinese. The broad-seated ribbonback chair continues to be popular and depending on style, age and condition a chair like this could be worth several thousand dollars at auction. At a recent auction we sold a reproduction 20th century Chippendale six-piece chair set for $900. I think people are drawn to the elegant and stately style of these pieces.

Duncan Phyfe. In the late 1700s and early 1800s Duncan Phyfe furniture was all the rage in Europe and New York. Characterized by straight line designs most pieces were made of hard woods such as mahogany and walnut. Today, an original piece in good condition could sell for tens of thousands of dollars and even the reproductions do well at auction.

Mission Style. In the late 19th century the Spanish missions through-out colonial California gave rise to a new, simpler style of furniture – Mission. Think of the oak desks, tables, cabinets and other pieces that feature vertical and horizontal lines and flat panels. Auction results for these original pieces have been quite strong. Makers like Gustav Stickley and Lambert are the serious performers.

French Country. Here's a style of furniture that always seems to do well. Drawing from a mix of influences from when Louis XIV, Louis XV, and Louis XVI reigned this style exemplifies casual, yet sophisti-cated living. You too can incorporate chateau style décor in your home if the price is right. At auction, you could see pieces like these go for several thousand dollars as well.

Whenever these antique pieces of furniture pass through our auction house I'm always amazed at how well many of them have stood the test of time. It really speaks volumes about the masterful craftsmanship.

Art Deco Style Personifies A Trend Toward Minimalism

In the auction world, or the secondary market, as it's often referred to we see many trends in purchasing. These are often of generational or even regional tastes, but the love for a particular style tends to be shorter lived. Let me just put it as, "What's in vogue this week?" or "What is New York telling us to like this season?"

Few of these styles seem to have the staying power of the Art Deco period. Often characterized by its bold stylized geometric forms and extravagant ornamentation, Art Deco was all the rage in the 1920s and 1930s after the world embraced Art Nouveau. I just always think of its simple straight lines. For me, black, white and silver or all things between World War I and World War II come to mind. Simplistic of me, yes, but also a helpful association.

A great example of Art Deco recently crossed the auction block and reminded me of the universal love for this style. It was a 1937 triangle shaped Swiss Omega desk clock that featured its original case and was in good working order. After the bidding ended and the clock realized $900, I thought to myself, "Wow, deco is still in." I say this as in my nearly two decades of reselling for clients I feel I've seen all styles come and go. However, Art Deco seems to always be cool. I see it on *Mad Men*, the television series based in the 1950s and 1960s and everything hip about that period. I saw it in the 1980s with *Miami Vice* and pop artist Patrick Nagel whose minimalist illustrations of women in *Playboy* and on Duran Duran's *Rio* album cover helped define that era. I saw it in the *Saturday Night Fever* album cover and again in the design of most things having to do with the 2000 Millennium, Disney's *Tron*, all things *Star Wars* and even Pac-Man. All of theese have several elements of Art Deco!

Currently, I credit the minimalist movement for this trend. With the simplistic designs of Art Deco it fits the mid-modernist and the minimalist trends of today's hip and downsizing Baby Boomers. It also goes with all Apple products. Yes a little joke, but seriously my iPhone 6 Plus looks deco to me. Now that begs the question, "Where is my triangular Apple iPhone?"

Trends in style, design and architecture come and go, but Art Deco seems to stay. Lately we are seeing even the most contemporary of furniture and jewelry incorporate this now classic style.

Now, if only I could invent the next best thing in a minimalist style. I'll have to channel my 10th grade geometry class to help me. It was "totally" Art Deco. To the max.

It's Been Avoided Long Enough... Art?

Next to the often-awkward estate furniture discussion: art is one of the most challenging conversations to have with a family in transition. Whether it's a painting that's been in the family for generations, a past art gallery purchase or a treasured find from years past all the forces are at play here. You may have family legend, price anchor or one of my favorite misconceptions, "It's old, so it's worth a lot." And another, "I bought this in the 1960s for X so it's done nothing but appreciate since then." All appraisers, auctioneers and estate sale experts deal with this every day.

I must explain that researching most art is like comping a house. We research similar works by that artist and see what they have sold for on the secondary market over the past few years. When I say similar I mean if it's an oil painting by an artist, I look for other oil paintings by that same artist. Further, if it's a portrait I look for other portraits in oil by that artist and then of the same size. Was it done at a time in the artist's life when he was prominent or early in his career? We look for it to be as close to matching the same style of work, in the same medium, of a similar dimension, executed at the same time as other examples. When this can't be done exactly, if say the artist wasn't prolific, an educated guess comes in to play based on the factors you do have.

Let me be clear here. If your artist does not have previous history of sales the price realized will be based on an eye of the beholder, a roll of the dice in the secondary market. You often cannot create interest where there is none. An artist that's been dead for 100 years and has no auction records is like a street artist selling his works at a parking lot sale. Many are amazing at their craft, but until established valuations are difficult. Just because you bought a painting from a charming street vendor for $5,000 does not make the market think it was worth what you paid. In all likelihood, it's worth about $300 when you walk out of the tent with it under your arm.

Is Your Artist An A-Lister?

The world of fine art is a strange land to most and especially when it comes to its resale and performance on the fair market. The most common question I'm asked is, "What's my art worth?" It's generally one of the most difficult questions to answer.

There are so many factors, but first and foremost is the artist. I hate to say it, but 99 times out of 100 a name is more important than the work and its execution. It's kind of sad to me. I have seen amazing desert landscapes

by an unknown "unlisted" artist sell for a few hundred dollars and a poor-
ly-executed desert landscape sell for tens of thousands by the right name.

What makes a name or an A-listed artist? It's an artist who has consistent
auction records or a solid trend of performance when resold on the open
market. Supply and demand are definitely factors too, but those resale
trends show the art collector, dealer and connoisseur that they are making
a sound investment.

The asking prices at a gallery or an online outlet rarely influence the resale
ability of a work of art. I've seen Picasso lithographs, Salvador Dali prints
and Andy Warhol serigraphs that have sold for $30,000 to $50,000 at
local galleries realize a fraction both at local and international auctions.
There was an implied investment value by the galleries, but the secondary market often proves otherwise. Factors need to be considered, such as
how many editions were created of the same piece, was the work executed
before the death of the artist and is it what the artist was known for? A
great name may not mean much if it is a tired piece that was reissued
hundreds of times.

Take Salvador Dali's limited-edition etching entitled "Autumn." Galleries offer this piece for $3,000 to $5,000. In October 2015, we sold this piece for $275. This auction had 7,500 approved bidders from 62 countries and was heavily advertised. This was the fair market and what the world deemed it to be worth. I just found another that sold in Tampa for $120. It's not the economy. It's supply and demand. There's a large supply, several hundred have been produced and not a piece that's in demand. People see Dali and remember hearing multi-million-dollar record sales and think, wow what a great investment.

Many people buy art because it speaks to them, but if you're looking to buy art as an investment do your homework. You might discover a nice find. One of my favorite things is when I get to tell a consignor they have a very valuable painting that they inherited. A lesser-known artist to the laymen, but to the art world a little piece of gold. I call these lottery tickets. You may have one, so I will not discourage anyone from finding out if you have that "A-List" artist.

4 Art Legends And Misnomers

I told you I was going to beat up on art, and here it goes as I address the most common, let's say confusion, I hear in the resale business.

The artist just died, so it's gone up in value. To answer bluntly, no. I give you Thomas Kincaid to illustrate my point. Should be a mic drop, but to explain further it's just demand. Yes the supply has been cut off, but is there any demand? Death has renewed interest in items for a short period of time, but generally more regarding pop culture items. Take for example, the short spike in the price of a Michael Jackson doll after his death.

It's unlike anything else the artist has ever painted, so it's worth more. I used to be this guy. I thought it would be common sense. You have a desired artist and something they did unusual and therefore, rare. That dirty word rare. I know I've already said that rare doesn't mean valuable unless there's demand. So, it's not true at all. Collectors will pay top dollar for only the paintings that are the best examples of what the artist is best known for. Auction records show that collectors have paid up to $50,000,000 for a Monet landscape, but $500,000 for a Monet portrait. Big difference.

It's the biggest painting by the artist, so it's worth more than smaller works. Rarely, if ever true because of all the other factors stated and in fact a painting can be too big. If you have an institutional sized painting you limit your bidder and buying pool as the average house can't fit or display some of these monumental works. Less interested parties generally mean less value or demand.

It's on canvas, so it must be a painting. Giclees and other new printing processes are getting so good that it's hard to tell for a novice. You may think you have just bought an original painting by a master, when surprise… it's a print on canvas. Not a forgery, that's different. It's a glori-fied print of a famous painting that is perfectly legal to replicate.

Now To Give You Nightmares

I can't talk about art without talking about fakes and forgeries. I'd like to say it wasn't common, but it's actually getting worse in our industry. 60 Minutes did a great exposé a few years ago as did 20/20. They interviewed forgers about their methods and the tricks of trade. They showed everything from using period canvas, mixing paints with a chemist's precision to match the masters' formulas to creating a false provenance and forging certification documents. It all seems high-tech and new, but I assure you this is nothing new and it has been going on since paintings were valued. It's what makes an old painting in a family, say 200 years old, difficult to tell. If it's a 200-year-old forgery everything will look right, have aged right and without the use of highly trained experts fool 90 percent of the art world. What this has done has flipped the art world upside down. Everything is now guilty until proven innocent. We find a nice painting in an estate where everything looks right, we put it online and the comments come pouring in. "It's fake," they say. Immediately the world jumps to the assumption that it's fake. It used to be so frustrating, but now I completely understand. We have been fooled several times and my staff has several experts. We now should be pessimists as well.

We have received paintings on consignment with provenance, certificates of authenticity and previous auction records that later have turned out to be forgeries or worse, just cast in doubt with no real answer. Our auction house is not alone. All the internationally-famous auction houses have been burned too. No one is unscathed. It's very frustrating and now we must change our listings of all works to, "In the Manner of" or "Attributed to." We can't be sure of most anything unless we can ask the artist or their heirs, or hope we find the piece in a catalog raisonné (of the known works) of the artist.

For the past year and a half, literally --18 plus months -- our company has been painstakingly researching one painting we are representing for an estate. I believe this journey will be the next book I keep alluding to. We have researched what we could ourselves. We have hired several private investigators along the way. We have contacted international experts and spoken to living artists that knew the owner. Most recently we've done forensic testing all to get to the bottom of one painting's authenticity. We are over $50,000 into the journey so far and it's all based on an original, educated guess, an initial gut feeling and a little junior detective work.

As you can see in this real-life illustration of what needs to be done to authenticate art when you are not sure is hardly worth it for most of the paintings in the world. So, how do you uncover a fake, $5,000 painting if it looks like a duck and quacks like a duck? You sure won't spend $50,000 to find out if it's worth $5,000. It's a challenge for everyone in the art world right now. If you're selling just know that it may be hard to authenticate your art. If you're buying, keep in mind that when you see "In the Manner of" and "Attributed to" that means there's no guarantee it is an original.

Done with art yet? As I always say buy it because you like it and want it to beautify your home or office. If you are buying it as an investment, caveat emptor. That's the only Latin I think know. Oh wait... Shakira, Gloria Estefan, E pluribus Unum.... it's all coming back to me.

Let's leave art and get in to selling methods, pros, cons and more.

SELLING?

So here you are, somewhat educated by my writings and ramblings. You find yourself downsizing, settling a loved one's estate or assisting a friend in the process. You have several options and don't know what's best for you. Are you a control freak, micromanager? Do you not want to be bothered and let someone else do it? Is your time more valuable than stressing about it? As with anything if you are educated you'll make a much better decision.

I will discuss several methods; my personal favorite is auction as it's what I do, but I do believe they all have their merits. These are my opinions and I have friends in these industries, so no offense if any of you disagree with me.

Yard Sales

Garage Sale, Yard Sale, Tag Sale, no matter what you call it this is a great way to sell that home overflow. Downsizers like it. Control freaks like it. Outgoing extroverts like it. You get to talk to everyone! You get to price everything at what you think is fair. If it's your house and your stuff I see nothing wrong with it. Where I stress caution is when you are doing it for an estate or helping a parent or a grandparent. What you see as yard sale junk might be the Holy Grail. I used to make a very good living yard sailing. Buying something for $5 and selling it a few days later on eBay for $500. I know an entire subculture of people who are doing this for a living. Feasting on your lack of knowledge. Again, if it's your old skis, clothes, gym equipment and other items like that, no worries. Mom's dolls, Dad's old cameras or stereo system, be careful. Ask your friends and try to get an expert just to have a look before you put it out for sale. Be careful please.

eBay, Craigslist And The Gang

As I said earlier, I used to make a living selling on eBay. It was a wonderful, fun way to sell things and downsizers liked it too. As eBay moved away from the strictly- auction thing and Buy-It Now was introduced, once again you could name your price like a yard sale with a much larger audience. Craigslist, Etsy and now even Facebook have similar functions. I liked the old eBay for the fact that, if you didn't know what you had the auction method of bidding would sniff out your lack of knowledge and generally solve it with crazy high bids. Basically a few collector experts would bid against each other and show you what the fair market "real value" was. A flat price doesn't do that. However, eBay does let you search sold item records so you can educate yourself to the asking price if you go with the flat price method. All these online platforms have their merits and simply the vast buyer base for you to expose your items to makes it a great avenue.

Just to touch on Craigslist horror stories. I know they are scary, but I think many become urban legend. It's been good for many to sell tools, furniture, workout equipment and cars. There are Craigslist tire kickers as I call them. Just answering ads to really see what else you have that you are selling and unknowledgeable about. This means you post a boat for sale and they come over and try to buy your silver flatware set or mother's jewelry. You get the analogy.

Estate Sale Companies

These companies generally employ experts to price your things and can handle everything for you. From the staging, valuations, staffing the sale days to the cleanout and removal they are a viable option for some people. Many are turnkey -- you don't have to do a thing but get out of the way. Based on your market, many are a terrific solution and you can get referrals from past clients. With an estate sale it's scheduled generally over a weekend beginning Friday, continuing Saturday and then many in our area have half-price Sunday. Many have a clause in the contract that whatever doesn't sell will be removed and donated or they will negotiate a lump sum buyout of the balance of goods. It's a great thing if you want an empty house to list. Real estate agents often refer estate sale companies for just this reason. However, I find for high-end and unique items the next method is better.

The Auction Method

I feel that the auction method, when executed properly, is the best method of selling on the secondary market overall. What do I mean by properly? My opinion is to catalog everything, list all items with photos on the Internet for advertising and bidding and invite the entire world to the offerings. At the end of the day, or auction, overall prices realized should be the fair market value of the goods. Some prices will be soft, some will be crazy, but they will average out and better yet, everything should be liquidated. The high-end and unique items when exposed to the world for bidding will garner the attention and bidders they deserve. People have comfort with estate sales in regard to that dreaded furniture. They can put a price tag on it and may even sell a few pieces, but what control they gain with furniture and other large items they lose on the valuable smalls and collectibles that must be priced to sell that weekend for wholesale prices. Many estate sales must cater to dealers to make sure everything moves. That said, so do auctions. I am just auction-biased and must admit, I have recommended that customers use estate companies when the circumstances for success look better for them.

I want to elaborate more into auctions as you may see why I have a passion for it.

Auction Psychology 101

If you're the type of person who likes to "people watch" then you'll be fascinated with the various personalities you'll find at an auction and what I call "Auction Psychology." Here in Arizona there's no lack of automobile auctions, business liquidation auctions, estate "on-site" auctions, real estate auctions and general merchandise auction houses. There seems to be a subculture here and the people who attend auctions often don't tell their friends. I am sure the psychology behind this stems from a fear that their friends have similar tastes and may bid against them which conjures up the adage, "There are no friends at an auction."

My favorite example of the mindset of buyers happens when there is rain, sleet or snow. Everyone thinks no one will be going, so if they brave the weather and attend the auction they will get amazing bargains. I have seen record prices set in 12 inches of snow. I myself, have fallen for this trick of Mother Nature several times in my life. Never seeming to learn, but that's the fun of it. One of the first auctions I conducted in Phoenix was in the pouring rain and we were packed. I told the family not to worry, assuring them it would work to their advantage. I knew nothing about the Phoenix market and was basing it off snow in Pennsylvania, but wow, it worked. Makes me want to open a tent auction during Monsoon Season. Probably a horrible idea.

Another common occurrence I have been seeing as of late happens when there are two of the same thing in the same auction. A recent example was two signed Greg Maddox baseballs. The first one sold for $90 and then the second sold for $130. No difference. Both were certified, signed at the same time and were in the same condition. Why do I find this odd? The trend used to be the other way with the first item selling higher. Might be a trend, but the psychology fascinates me.

Then there's an auctioneer's favorite, "I want it, and don't want anyone else to have it at any price." You'll see this most often in art, firearms and jewelry auctions. I've seen it at tool and furniture auctions as well. A man will buy a ladder for $50 more than they cost at Home Depot because he's mad at a bidder who outbid him on a shop vac. It's quite a thing to see. Two billionaires sparring with bidder paddles over a Picasso or two ladies over a Tiffany bracelet. But just so you know, if this was the normal occurrence at an auction no one would attend or everyone would be an auctioneer.

The bidder tricks, the poker faces and overall gamesmanship are all part of the Auction Psychology. It's fun to watch and even more exciting to partic-ipate. Try it sometime, you'll see why so many of us are hooked!

BUYING?

Why Young People Should Collect Now

If you were born 20 to 30 years ago consider yourself lucky because time is on your side. I'm not talking about opening a savings account; rather I'm referring to your chance to make smart investments in the secondary market.

Generational collector trends show us he who buys now will greatly profit later. In today's auction world the paradigms of the past have shifted. What was hot is not. Whole new avenues have opened in collections. Values in general have been greatly been diminished. As it was in the 1920s and the 1960s when no one wanted old things, the past has repeated. Here we are again in a similar cycle where valuable furniture, antiques and other collectibles are selling for a fraction of their value years ago. Those who were smart enough to purchase during those lulls greatly profited in their collections later.

This is something I can attest to personally as my parents were avid antique collectors. They traveled often in the 1960s purchasing a variety of treasures. When they would speak to me in values of which they purchased these items I did not understand the method behind their madness. But when they went to sell these items in the 1980s and 1990s the return on the items astounded me. I am seeing the same trend today and I now understand why growing collections and understanding the underappreciated value currently will return tenfold.

I often hear the antique market is dead as the millennial generation does not see or understand the true value of great antiques. So, if you fall into this age group why should you care?

Here are four reasons why you should take a second look at buying on the secondary market:

Most antique and collectible markets have reached rock bottom.

This is the largest transfer of wealth in human history.

Collectibles are cyclical.

The Baby Boomers are the largest generation to move into transition in U.S. history.

We live in a high-tech world that is going to advance even further. I believe that as this technology frees up more of our time some of life's formalities will come back. We're already seeing some of this with the Steampunk movement which takes its inspiration from the 19th century Victorian Age. Antique timepieces, old typewriters, vintage lamps, old maps, jewelry or décor with ornate engravings... it's just a matter of time before we see more people serving dinner with fine china.

I'm no psychic, but I know trends are cyclical. If I were 20 years younger right now I'd be researching these cycles and looking for great finds at yard sales, antique stores and auctions.

So, all of this said to you and you are still not a collector or thinking of investing in stuff, it's okay. Buy Tesla stock.

Buying Someone Something Cool

I've always found the psychology of gift giving fascinating, especially at the holidays or birthdays. Most of us have that one relative who is notorious for re-gifting and the White Elephant gift exchange at work typically features some oddball items.

Stocking stuffers I think are always underrated and many people choose to fill the stockings with inexpensive items like a chocolate Santa or a trinket. Why not surprise your loved one this year with a small, but collectible gift that will have value for years to come?

Here are some ideas for you.

> **Carved Jade.** Asian collectibles continue to be hot. We've seen this trend for the past three years and it shows no sign of slowing down. A carved jade pendant, figurine, plaque or small bowl would surely be a treasured surprise inside a Christmas stocking. After all, many people believe jade has magical qualities.

Collectible Coins. Coins have always been solid, even during the recession. Things to take into consideration include rarity, how many coins were in the mintage, whether the coin is silver or gold, distinct symbols and even errors made on the coin. My suggestion for a stocking stuffer? A Morgan silver dollar with a Carson City mint mark or any coin with a low mintage.

Anything Art Deco. Whether it's a piece of costume jewelry or a fountain pen you can't go wrong with Art Deco gifts. Often characterized by its bold stylized geometric forms and extravagant ornamentation, Art Deco was all the rage in the 1920s and 1930s after the world embraced Art Nouveau. Nearly 100 years later, it's still popular.

Perfume Bottles. What if you wow your loved one with a vintage perfume bottle? Bottles by Tiffany, Lalique, Steuben and Baccarat should continue to hold their value in years to come. They have been desired by collectors since their inception and make powerful keepsakes.

Vintage Knives. A vintage pocket or folding knife can be a great little gift for anyone who appreciates the craftsmanship behind the blades, handles and overall functionality. Collecting knives became popular during the 1960s when the U.S. began requiring knife manufacturers to mark their knives with the country of origin. Brands to look for include Buck, Camillus, Case, Queen, Randall, Remington, Schrade and Winchester. Also, there are some amazing custom makers who truly produce works of art.

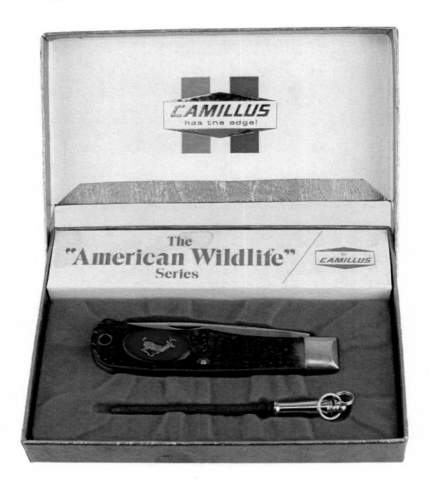

Of course, you could always include a Christmas ornament in a stocking and certain antique ornaments like Waterford, Dresden, Kugel and even Hallmark still do well at auction. Or you could go for something more modern like an Elf on the Shelf. Will kids from today pay top dollar for this silly elf 40 years from now? If only we could ask the Ghost of Christmas' Yet to Come!

Other Gifts Worth Buying On The Secondary Market

I am going to get you to buy something at a yard sale, estate sale or auction by the end of this book. Since we all have that loved one or friend who is impossible to shop for try the secondary market. Be it odd, bizarre or just outside the box I like my gifts to be different, memorable, funny or just plain thought-provoking.

Where do I get my gifts? Nine times out of 10 at an estate auction. Sometimes something triggers a memory and I'll try eBay if I can't find an item at the local auctions, antique or thrift stores. People always love the thought behind the gift. Sure gift cards are safe, but not much thought goes into that. TVs and computers are cool, but passé tomorrow.

Here are six more ideas to help you surprise someone:

> **For the man child friend.** He›s 40, acts like he›s 12 and you've been buds forever. Go with a childhood favorite toy. Get him a 1980s carded He-Man figure for about $100 on eBay or at a toy auction. It's still appreciating in value and it will make for a great conversation piece.

For the woman in your life. Surprise her with estate jewelry. The price you pay for a vintage beauty at a fine estate sale will be one-tenth of retail. We often find vintage Tiffany, Cartier and many with their original boxes. Imagine a 1930s Art Deco diamond cocktail ring with stories to tell, selling for $300 to $500. Beat that, Jared.

For your special man. You can't go wrong with a vintage watch. Not only are they in style, but you'll find all price ranges and they can be a solid investment. You'll be surprised at how much more affordable they are at auction or at an estate sale than retail, plus so much cooler.

For the avid reader. Sorry iPad and Kindle peeps, but a classic, first edition, leather-bound book can be an amazing present. I once gave a friend an early edition of Bram Stoker's Dracula and he still has it on his mantle 20 years later. It was $35 at an estate auction.

For the car buff. A classic car may sound crazy, but watch the local car auctions. You often can find that old Mustang he had in high school for $5,000 today. Plus, it will give the family a project.

For a good friend or colleague. Go with something unusual. The sky's the limit when it comes to this genre at an estate sale or auction. I have found mounted insects and bats, bizarre medical devices, vintage board games, old typewriters and even that special childhood lunchbox can make a great gift. I once gave a 19th century brass microscope to a doctor friend of mine. He cried and said it was the coolest thing he ever received in his life. I paid about $85.

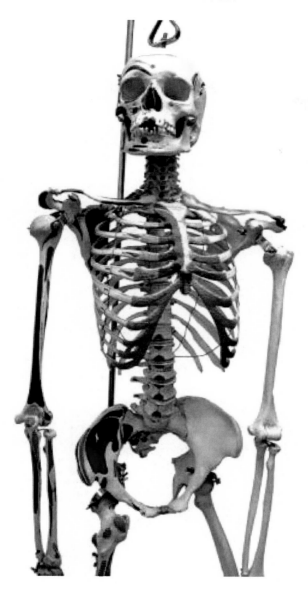

This year, I hope you give real thought to finding special gifts for family and friends you care about. The rest can have gift cards and a new flat screen.

A FINAL WORD

I want to come back to the initial question so many of you ask, "Why don't they want my stuff?" I hope you now have insight into the many, many whys and have learned a few things to educate yourself. If you are a Boomer reading this book you can stop being frustrated with your children. If you are a Gen X'er you can stop being amazing, oh wait, I flatter my generation...stop being stuck in the middle. Does this make us the Jan Brady Generation? Okay Millennials, maybe I made collectors out of three percent of you and helped you understand your parents and grandparents. Seriously, I'd love feedback from you Millennials and even Gen Z. I have an idea of what you think is cool to collect now, but what do you think you'll collect 10 years from now?

A Few Of My Favorite Cheesy, Spoof Reviews

"I am moved to say, Josh Levine may be the worst writer of our Generation."

"Nonfiction has a new threat."

"Mr. Levine's beanie babies, Hummels & herpes reference sounds like a personal experience."

"If this man were to write what would obviously be a self-published sequel I am hoping no trees would be harmed by receiving the toxin that would be their printed words."

"If I could give this book a 1 star review I would, but Mr. Levine would most likely try to sell it."

"This author should try writing about something he personally knows about, like mullets."

"The ignorant may have a new champion. Look out Glenn Beck."